STONEHENGE AND THE GREAT PYRAMID:

WINDOW ON THE UNIVERSE

Stonehenge and the Great Pyramid:

WINDOW ON THE UNIVERSE

A search for the secrets of the universe
and the origin of creation.

by
Bonnie Gaunt

Dedicated to
the
Creator of the Universe;
and a recognition
of his
power and majesty.

Foreword
and
Acknowledgements

"Thou hast ordered all things in measure and number and weight," *(Wisdom of Solomon, The Apocrypha).* The Alexandrian who wrote those words shortly before the Christian era expressed a profound truth. Number is indeed the foundation principle in all creation.

In this work, I hope to open for the reader, the joy and beauty of the language of number. I have attempted to examine the evidence for the existence of an intelligent Creator—an interwoven pattern of number in all of His realm—and an exploration into the very core of creation. I invite the reader to share this journey with me—a journey to the place of beginning.

My sincere appreciation is given to Neil Pinter, Priest River, Idaho, for his encouragement and contribution to this study. A special thanks to Mark Burke, Colonial Press, Inc., Jackson, Michigan, for his kindness in freely granting me the use of the computer for typesetting; and to Terry Johnson, for her generous work of proofreading. Most of all, my loving appreciation to the great God of the universe, who permitted me to catch a fleeting glimpse of the beauty of His realm.

Bonnie Gaunt
Jackson, Michigan, U.S.A., 1993

CONTENTS

The Great Pyramid—the wonder of the ancient world—contains, within its silent stones, the mysteries of the universe.

Photo by Todd Alexander

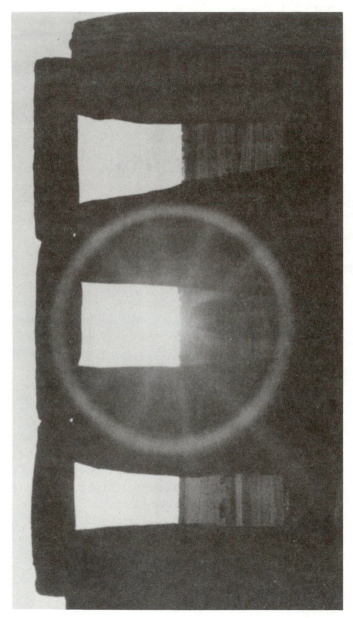

More than a million sunrises have cast their warmth over the mute stones of Stonehenge, and today, the sun at the summer solstice still rises over the Heelstone, appearing as a golden crown upon its ancient head.

1
The Language of the Universe

In A.D. 1963, astronomers in Green Bank, West Virginia pointed a giant saucer-shaped antenna at two remote stars, *Tau Ceti* and *Epsilon Eridani.* They were indeed listening for a message from outer space.

These were not visionary amateurs. The project was a sincere attempt to receive a message—if one were there—from extraterrestrial beings.

If such un-earthly beings did exist, and if they did attempt to communicate to earthlings, what language would they use? After pondering the problem, they concluded that the only language that would make sense to all intelligent forms of life, anywhere in the universe, would be a mathematical one.

Mathematics, they said, is not so much a body of knowledge as it is a special kind of language—one so perfect and abstract that it could be understood by any intelligent creatures, existing anywhere. The grammar of the language is simple logic, and the vocabulary of the language are simple symbols—basically, numerals, that represent numbers.

As children we were taught numerals as if they were dead symbols of amount. Their function as a language was not part of our journey through the three R's. Thus, their function as language does not find in us a response of recognition. And for this we are the poorer.

Not so in ancient times. Pythagoras, the 5th century B.C. mathematician said "Numbers are the language of the universe." And he taught his students their importance as a

1

language. Indeed, numbers are the very building blocks of creation—but they are more than this. They are a language that communicates through time and space—an external language—a language of beginning.

Plato perceived the language of numbers and some of its messages planted in the universe. And he was aware of its source. "God ever geometrizes," he wrote. Sir James Jeans, the British physicist declared, "The Great Architect of the universe now begins to appear as a pure mathematician."

He does not send us a "beep-beep-beep" or a "dot-dot-dash" from somewhere in the heavens, but he has left his great catalog of sacred information for us, concealed in number, planted in the universe, and in his written word.

> *To whom then will ye liken God? or what likeness will ye compare to him...? Have ye not known? Have ye not heard? Hath it not been told you from the beginning? Have ye not understanding from the foundation of the earth? It is he that sitteth upon the circle of the earth...; that stretcheth out the heavens as a curtain, and spreadeth them out as a tent to dwell in.... Lift up your eyes on high, and behold who hath created these things, that bringeth out their host by number...* (Isaiah 40:18-26)

In the writings of the ancient philosophers there is common agreement that the purpose of number is for the investigation of the universe. From the atom to the galaxy in the heavens, the same unchanging laws apply—the laws of arithmetic, the language of number.

Just as the hand of God spread the vast expanse of the heavens by number, so too his written word can be reduced to number; and those who have tried it have stood in awe of the intricacy and beauty of its design. It was an intentional design.

In the year 547 B.C. a man named Daniel, a Hebrew captive in Babylon, was given a vision which carried him into the vast unknown future. At the conclusion of the vision he saw two un-earthly creatures who spoke concerning the time when the vision would be fulfilled. One of these creatures was identified by the name *Palmoni*. It is a Hebrew word which means The Wonderful Numberer, or the Numberer of Secrets. Daniel, being a Hebrew, would have been aware of the importance of the name. He was also aware of the language of number that was a vital part of his native tongue.

Hebrew is probably the oldest language known to man. It was a "dual character system"—a meaning of sound and a meaning of number. It is the language of the Old Testament. Thus that wonderful old book, owned by nearly every Christian the world over, is not only an historical record of man's relationship with his Creator, it is also a storehouse of secrets, locked up in number. The Numberer of Secrets who spoke to Daniel knew and used the language of number, the language of the universe.

The New Testament was also written in a dual character system—the Greek language. The Greeks called this system *gematria*.[1]

Gematria among the Greeks was in common use at the time of the writing of the New Testament. A copy of one of these early manuscripts, called *papyri,* (because they were written on papyrus) exists today in Dublin, Ireland in the Chester Beatty Collection. It is dated somewhere between 200 and 300 A.D. This manuscript uses gematria for every number in the book of Revelation, rather than Arabic numerals as we have in our modern translation. For example, every time the number 7 appears, it is written as ζ, which is the letter *zeta,* having a number value of 7.

These number codes have been known and used through time. One of the best known demonstrations of gematria in the

---

1 The Hebrew term for gematria, if there ever was one, is apparently lost. The closest thing to it is Rule No. 29 of the 32 rules in the *Baraita* for studying the Torah.

Old Testament is the section headings in Psalm 119. Any student of the Old Testament is aware that the names for these sections are in fact the sequential letters of the Hebrew alphabet. Not so well known is the fact that each stanza begins with the letter-number of its particular section. For instance, in section א (aleph - 1) each stanza begins with א, and this pattern continues throughout each section, using ultimately all twenty-two letters of the Hebrew alphabet.

In more modern times, the noted Bible expositor, E. W. Bullinger was among the many who have added to our understanding of the subject of gematria. His book *Number in Scripture,* published in 1894, shows the supernatural design in the use of numbers, both in the works of God and in the word of God. Closely following his work was the brilliant expose' of the science of gematria by William Stirling in his book, *The Canon,* first published in 1897. He showed the undeniable connection between the gematria of the Bible and the geometry of the universe. In the decade of the 1920s, author Frederick Bligh Bond increased the world's awareness of this ancient science by his works, *The Apostolic Gnosis,* and *Gematria.* Another expositor, Ivan Panin, published his *Bible Numerics* articles in 1912. More recently published is the work of Jerry Lucas and Del Washburn, *Theomatics* (Stein & Day, New York, 1977). In fact, the number equivalents for the Greek and Hebrew languages can be found in any Webster's Dictionary.

The Greek alphabet uses 24 letters. Their number values are as follows:

Alpha	α	1
Beta	β	2
Gamma	γ	3
Delta	δ	4
Epsilon	ε	5
Zeta	ζ	7
Eta	η	8
Theta	θ	9
Iota	ι	10
Kappa	κ	20
Lambda	λ	30
Mu	μ	40
Nu	ν	50
Xi	ξ	60
Omicron	o	70
Pi	π	80
Rho	ρ	100
Sigma	$\sigma . \varsigma$	200
Tau	τ	300
Upsilon	υ	400
Phi	φ	500
Chi	χ	600
Psi	ψ	700
Omega	ω	800

Originally their alphabet contained 26 letters, however two have fallen out of use through time. These letters stood for the numbers 6 and 90. The only use of the symbol for 6 in the New Testament is in Revelation 13:18 when giving the number of the beast. In the original manuscript, this number was written in gematria, using the three letters $\chi\xi\varsigma'$, which stand for 600, 60, and 6 respectively.

The Hebrew alphabet uses 22 letters, with the addition of extended characters for some of the finals. In other words, if a character appeared within a word it would be written differently than if it appeared at the end of a word. These finals were given alternative numbers. However, in my study of the use of Hebrew as a numbering system, I find very little use of the alternate numbers for finals. The number equivalents for the Hebrew alphabet are as follows:

א	'Aleph	....	1
ב	Bêyth	....	2
ג	Gîymel	....	3
ד	Dâleth	....	4
ה	Hê'	....	5
ו	Vâv	....	6
ז	Zayin	....	7
ח	Chêyth	....	8
ט	Têyth	....	9
י	Yôwd	....	10
כ, final ך	Kaph	....	20
ל	Lâmed	....	30
מ, final ם	Mêm	....	40
נ, final ן	Nûwn	....	50
ס	Çâmek	....	60
ע	'Ayin	....	70
פ, final ף / פ	Phê' / Pê'	....	80
צ, final ץ	Tsâdêy	....	90
ק	Qôwph	....	100
ר	Rêysh	....	200
שׁ / שׂ	Sîyn / Shîyn	....	300
ת / ת	Thâv / Tâv	....	400

As an example of how this numbering system works, let's look at the best known name in the New Testament—the Lord Jesus Christ. The gematria for his name is demonstrated thus:

K	=	20	I	=	10	X	=	600
υ	=	400	η	=	8	ρ	=	100
ρ	=	100	σ	=	200	ι	=	10
ι	=	10	o	=	70	σ	=	200
o	=	70	υ	=	400	τ	=	300
s	=	200	s	=	200	o	=	70
		800			888	s	=	200
								1480

Lord	=	800
Jesus	=	888
Christ	=	1480
		3168

Jesus	=	888
Christ	=	1480
		2368

These are not random numbers. Their frequency of use both in the word of God and in the works of God is astounding.

The meaning of numbers is not an arbitrary assignment. A number only begins to reveal its meaning through use. The use of the number 8 throughout the gematria of the Old and New Testaments reveals its relationship to Jesus, the resurrection, and a new beginning. In fact the word "beginning" in Hebrew has the number equivalent of 8. The raising of a number to three identical digits shows the ultimate power in the meaning or function of the number. Thus the number 8, raised to three digits is Jesus, 888—the power and the means through which the resurrection and the new beginning for man can be accomplished.

All life on this earth is made possible by light from the sun. It takes 8 minutes for light from the sun to reach the earth.

Even the elements, of which all creation is made, attest to the universal use of numbers. The atomic number for the oxygen atom is 8. Oxygen is the very breath of life for man. Jesus said *"I am the life"*—the number value of the Greek letters is 888. Even the word *"life,"* in Greek, bears the number 808. He came to be the Saviour of mankind, and the word *"save"* in Greek is 8.

The prophecy concerning the birth of Jesus, as quoted by Matthew (Matt. 1:23) bears his number. *"Behold, a virgin shall concieve and bear a son, and shall call his name Emmanuel, which being interpreted is, God with us."* The number value of the Greek text is 8880.

7

Thirty three and one half years later (12,240 days), he was put to death on a cross, and laid in a grave. When grieving women went to his tomb, they found an angel there who announced to them, *"He lives."* That brief statement of the angels has the number value of 888.

Even the days of his life were a multiple of 8 (8 x 1,530 = 12,240).

The climax of Jesus' mission was stated by the Apostle Paul who declared, *"He must reign until he has put all enemies under his feet."* (I Cor. 15:25). What a joy to find the number value of that statement to be 8888.

These are no coincidences. Nor is it a matter of cut and fit to make the numbers work. These numbers are part of a plan so vast and so intricately interwoven into all creation that they can only speak of the incomprehensible mind of the Creator!

The name Lord Jesus Christ, *Κυριος Ιησους Χριστος* has the number value of 3168. The number has significance of immense proportions. Another title identifying him is used in I Timothy 2:5: *"Mediator between God and man,"* *μεσιτης Θεου και ανθρωπων,* which also has the number value of 3168. The number is three fifths of the British mile.

If we were to enclose the earth within a square, the perimeter of that square would be 31,680 miles.

Mean diameter of earth 7,920 miles.
Perimeter of square 31,680 miles.

That the gematria for the name Lord Jesus Christ should be planted in the geometry of the earth suggests a definite relationship between the gematria of the Bible and the geometry of the universe. They both speak the same language—the language of numbers.

Upon further examination of the geometry of our solar system we find the number repeated. The mean distance that light travels from the sun to the earth is 93 million miles. Dropping all the zeros, this distance would be 589,248 inches. If we were to divide this by the speed of light the result would be 3168 (589,248 ÷ 186 = 3,168).

The Encyclopedia Brittanica lists the mean distances from the sun to each of the nine planets thus (the zeros are left off as they are merely place holders):

Mercury	36
Venus	67
Earth	93
Mars	142
Jupiter	483
Saturn	886
Uranus	1782
Neptune	2793
Pluto	3672
Aggregate	9954

Thus the combined distances from the sun to each of the planets is 9954. If we were to take this figure as the circumference of a giant circle, the diameter of that circle would be 3168.

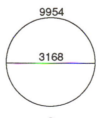

The name Lord Jesus Christ is planted in our solar system, coded in number.

But, you might say, didn't they discover a tenth planet out there beyond Pluto—Planet *X* ? For nearly a hundred years astronomers have been telling us that there is a Planet *X* out beyond Pluto. They have never seen it with their telescopes, but because of the unusual eliptic path of Uranus and Pluto they knew that a tenth planet was out there somewhere, affecting these orbits.

In the 1950s some astronomers suggested that instead of an unknown planet beyond Pluto, perhaps there existed a belt of huge ice chunks surrounding the solar system. They named it the Kuiper belt.

In August of 1992, a tiny reddish spot of light recorded on a sensitive electronic detector in Hawaii became the first component of the Kuiper belt ever observed. The existence of the Kuiper belt was suddenly changed from theory to fact. The new spot of light was named 1992 QB1.

Time magazine (September 28, 1992, p. 59) made the following observation about this discovery:

> Proof that the Kuiper belt exists would help demonstrate that another long-sought object almost certainly does not. For nearly a century, astronomers have been looking for a Planet X, a world conjectured to lie far beyond Pluto.... Planet X was first dreamed up to explain apparent irregularities in Neptune's orbit. Recent studies have shown those irregularities to be an illusion—and the sighting of QB1 has probably dashed forever the hope of finding a 10th planet.[1]

Why 9 planets? Why does the aggregate of their distances (9954) resolve to 9 (9 + 9 + 5 + 4 = 27 and 2 + 7 = 9)? Does the number 9 have any special significance?

---

1 Used by permission of Time, Inc., New York, NY.

According to mathematicians, 9 is the magic number. You can do things with 9, they say, that cannot be done with any other number. It represents completeness—wholeness of a concept—because 9 is the completion of the digits.

In the Old Testament, the Hebrew word for *perfection* has the number equivalent of 90. The word carries the thought of wholeness.

The existence of 9 planets tells us there is not a tenth—for 9 is wholeness or completeness; and their combined distances from the sun is a number that resolves to 9, further emphasizing their completeness. That number, when taken as the circumference of a circle gives a diameter of 3168—a number that also resolves to 9.

As we saw above, when a single digit number is raised to its triplet, it signifies that number raised to its ultimate or highest concept. Thus when we raise 9 to its triplet, 999, we come to the ultimate concept of creation—the one who created all things. The first four words of the Bible reveal that Creator. *"In the beginning God,"* בראשית אלהים, has a number value of 999.

Earth diameter	7,920 — 9
Sun diameter	864,000 — 9
Moon diameter	2,160 — 9

A square on each of these diameters would also resolve to 9.

Earth diameter	$7,920 \times 4 = 3,168$ — 9
Sun diameter	$864,000 \times 4 = 3,456,000$ — 9
Moon diameter	$2,160 \times 4 = 8,640$ — 9

A square drawn on each of these orbs makes a simple geometric figure of a square inscribed by a circle.

If that circle represented the earth, with its mean diameter of 7,920 miles, then the perimeter of the square would become 31,680 miles. The name Lord Jesus Christ has a number value of 3168.

A model of this relationship exists in the earth today. It is the four-thousand year old stone circles known as Stonehenge.

An outer circle of standing stones, known as the Sarsen Circle, surrounds an inner circle of smaller stones, called the Bluestone Circle. The mean circumference of the outer circle measures 316.8 feet, while the inner circle has a diameter of 79.2 feet.

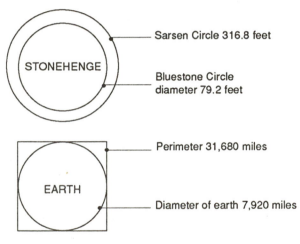

What does Stonehenge have to do with the geometry of the earth and with the Lord Jesus Christ? Is there an intended correlation, or is it an innocent coincidence?

Why Stonehenge?

2

Why Stonehenge?

Before dismissing the relationship of the Stonehenge measures to the earth as an innocent coincidence, let's take a look at another astounding relationship.

In the year A.D. 90, the Apostle John was given a vision while living in exile on the Isle of Patmos in the Mediterranean. One of the things he saw in that vision was a city; its measures and proportions he described thus:

> And the city lieth four-square, and the length is as large as the breadth: and he measured the city with the reed, twelve thousand furlongs. The length and breadth and the height of it are equal. And he measured the wall thereof, an hundred and forty and four cubits, according to the measure of a man." (Revelation 21:16-17)

The first measure was given in furlongs—660 feet—and the second measure was given in cubits. It becomes apparent when attempting to draw the geometric figure that John described, that the cubit used was the royal cubit of 1.72 feet.

Drawing the ground plan of this city produces a square inscribed by a circle. The dimension of this circle and square are precisely that of the Sarsen Circle and the Bluestone Circle at Stonehenge, but on a larger scale.

By disregarding the zeros and decimal points, the ground plan of one can be overlaid on the ground plan of the other and become identical. This in turn can be overlaid by the diagram of the earth with a square drawn on its circumference. The three configurations are identical in design and in number.

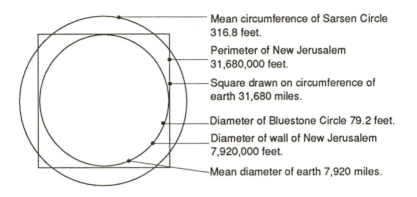

Mean circumference of Sarsen Circle 316.8 feet.

Perimeter of New Jerusalem 31,680,000 feet.

Square drawn on circumference of earth 31,680 miles.

Diameter of Bluestone Circle 79.2 feet.

Diameter of wall of New Jerusalem 7,920,000 feet.

Mean diameter of earth 7,920 miles.

The plurality of structures with a perimeter of 3168, the number value for Lord Jesus Christ, are quite apparent in the Old Testament. All of these structures have one common aspect—they were all designed by God.

Solomon's temple, built in Jerusalem had a base perimeter of ~~316.8 feet.~~[1] *3168 inches*

The Cities of Refuge each had a perimeter of 316,800 inches.[2]

---

1 According to I Kings 6:16 & 17, Solomon's Temple had a base perimeter of 160 cubits. In II Chronicles 7:3, Solomon was instructed to use the cubit of the "first measure"—that is, the old cubit, the Sumerian cubit of 19.8 inches. The 1972 edition of the Encyclopedia Judiaca (p. 947) gives a cubit of 19.8 inches as the measure used in the construction of Solomon's Temple.

2 The dimensions of the Cities of Refuge are given in Numbers 35:5, as 4,000 cubits for each side of the suburbs, giving a perimeter of 16,000 cubits. Using the "first measure"—the ancient Sumerian cubit that was popular at the time—the perimeter of the suburbs would be 316,800 British inches.

WHY STONEHENGE?

The city that the prophet Ezekiel saw in vision had a perimeter of 31,680 feet.[1]

If the Architect of the universe used this number repeatedly in his creation and in his instructions to man for the building of structures or cities, then we are naturally drawn to Stonehenge with wonder and awe. Was this structure also of divine origin?

What was Stonehenge? Why is the number value for Lord Jesus Christ planted in its ancient stone circles?

Theories about the origin and purpose of Stonehenge have been nearly as numerous as the centuries that have passed since its construction. Today it still stands stark and lonely on the Salisbury Plain in southern England.

Many legends have come down to us through the ages, and the mystery of those ancient monoliths still haunts the minds of all who have pondered their origin. The very sight of Stonehenge arouses a feeling of mystery and the supernatural—of a power and an intelligence greater than man.

---

1 The dimensions of Ezekiel's city are recorded in Ezekiel 48:35 as 18,000 measures. This special measure was given to Ezekiel in the vision and it was equivalent to 21.12 British inches, or 1.76 feet.

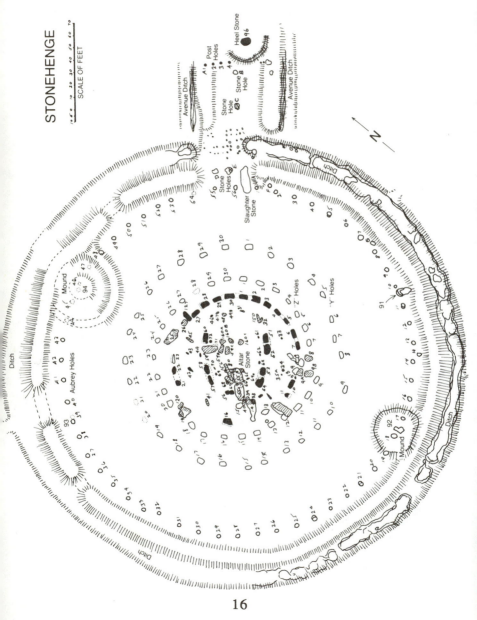

WHY STONEHENGE?

Stonehenge consists of several concentric circles, with two inner circles opened and spread to form U-shaped arrangements called "horseshoes." Out beyond the circles, toward the northeast, is a large natural boulder called the Heelstone.

The innermost arrangement of stones is called the Bluestone Horseshoe, because of the blueish color of the stones when wet. Outside the arrangement of bluestones, and dwarfing them in size stand the huge stones of the Trilithon Horseshoe. These are free-standing sets consisting of two uprights topped by a lintel. There are five of these trilithons. The name comes from *tri,* meaning three, and *lithos,* meaning stone. They form a U-shaped set of frames through which the sunrise, sunset, moonrise and moonset can be viewed at the equinoxes and solstices. Both the Bluestone and Trilithon Horseshoes are open toward the northeast, in the direction of sunrise.

Surrounding the trilithons is the Bluestone Circle. Only 20 of the original stones of this circle can be seen above ground today.

Immediately outside the Bluestone Circle is the Sarsen Circle. It was originally composed of 30 uprights, topped by 30 lintels. They are of sarsen, from whence it derives its name. The inner faces of these uprights were dressed and polished. The mean circumference of this most remarkable circle is 316.8 feet, corresponding to the number value of the name Lord Jesus Christ. The discovery of this relationship began to change the established thinking concerning the origin and purpose of Stonehenge.

Far out beyond the Sarsen Circle lies the Aubrey Circle. This is a circle of small holes, so named for their discoverer, John Aubrey, who found them in 1666. There are 56 holes in the circle, 32 of which have been covered with cement markers for purposes of identification by tourists.

Standing approximately on the line of the Aubrey Circle were four unhewn monoliths which formed the corners of a rectangle perpendicular to summer sunrise. Only two of these stones remain today, and one of them is lying on its face.

17

Surrounding the Aubrey Circle is a bank and ditch. This bank is thought to have been about six feet high and about twenty feet wide, forming an outer barrier or wall of the monument. The bank was composed of white chalk, which makes up most of the surface of the region around Stonehenge. It is supposed that this bank, as well as serving as a barrier for the enclosure, was also used as a horizon for viewing the sun and moon through the stone archways. There was a 35-foot opening in the bank at the entrance, facing the summer sunrise.

To the northeast of the circle is the Heelstone. It stands alone and separate from the stones of the circles, yet is a vital part of the monument, for it served as a marker for the sunrise at the summer solstice, when the sun was at its most northerly extreme. The name Heelstone was probably derived from the Greek, *helios,* meaning sun. The word *helios* has a number value of 318 and it is most interesting to find that a circle with a diameter of 318 will have a circumference of 999, corresponding to the first words of Genesis, *"In the beginning God,"* which has a number equivalent of 999.

The Heelstone is definitely the sun stone, for it stands outside the entrance, marking the northernmost extreme of the sun at the summer solstice. Some have suggested that it was the most important stone of the monument. This would be comparable to saying that the hands are the most important part of a clock. They are important indeed, but would point to nothing of value unless the remaining parts of the clock were functioning according to design.

The Heelstone does in fact still tell the time at Stonehenge. From the time of its construction over 4,000 years ago, the Heelstone still marks the time of the summer solstice.[1]

It has long been known that Stonehenge was oriented to the

---

1 The precession of the equinoxes, which moves the sun backward along the path of the ecliptic, has not separated the appearance of the sun from atop the Heelstone, and it still has about another 4,000 years before this connection would no longer happen.

Photo by Thomas Gilbert

The famous Heelstone or Sunstone. Some say its name is derived from the Greek "helios." meaning "sun."

summer solstice sunrise. In the 1950s, Professor Gerald Hawkins, an astronomer from Boston University, went to Stonehenge to observe the sunrise and the various sighting lines through the stone archways, collecting data which he brought back and programmed into an IBM 7090 computer. That marvellous achievement of modern man, the computer, was necessary to unlock the secrets, to unravel the mystery, and to unveil the beauty of Stonehenge. And beautiful it is, for it reveals a Creator whose plan for man reaches far into the future.

Thanks to the brilliant work of Hawkins and his "machine," the mystery of Stonehenge has begun to unfold, and the silent stones begin to speak.

In 1880, Wm. Flinders Petrie wrote that the rising of the summer solstice sun over the Heelstone was "mere coincidence."

As Hawkins began getting answers from his computer, he knew that it was no "mere coincidence"—it was planned precision. He had not been prepared for the overwhelming evidence. He found that 12 of the significant Stonehenge alignments pointed to an extreme position of the sun, and 12 alignments pointed to an extreme position of the moon.[1]

The relationship of Stonehenge to the sun and moon is awesome. Hawkins was so amazed at the sun and moon alignments at Stonehenge that he computed the probabilities. He found it to be ten million to one that those alignments could not have been by coincidence.

Since Hawkins' work, the discovery of the remarkable relationship of the mean circumference of the Sarsen Circle to the name Lord Jesus Christ has opened a whole new vista—a window on the universe.

Why was the number for Lord Jesus Christ used for the measurement of that circle of stones 2,000 years before he came to earth?

---

1 Gerald S. Hawkins, *Stonehenge Decoded,* Dell Publishing Co., New York, p. 107.

Not only do we find the number of his name in the circumference of the circle, it is also in the area contained within the circle. The area within that circle of 316.8 feet is 888 square yards. The name Jesus has the number value of 888.

These figures are derived by using British measures. I wondered what would happen if I used other ancient measures.

A unit found in the measuring of megalithic sites in England has been called the megalithic yard—abbreviated to MY. It is the equivalent of 2.72 British feet. If the mean circumference of the Sarsen Circle were measured by the megalithic yard, it would be 116.4 MY. It is no coincidence that 1164 is the number value for the title Son of God, υιος Θεου.

A unit of measure that had been given to the prophet Ezekiel for measuring the temple and city that he saw in the vision was called the reed. It was equivalent to 10.56 British feet. If we were to measure the mean circumference of the Sarsen Circle in reeds, it would be 29.99. The gematria for *"Thou art the Son of God,"* οτι συ ει ο υιος του Θεου, is 2999.

A well known ancient unit of measure was the royal cubit. It was the equivalent of 1.72 British feet. If we were to measure the mean diameter of the Sarsen Circle in royal cubits, it would be 586. The title, *Master,* by which Jesus was often addressed, has a number value of 586.

Other geometry of that circle of stones continues to yield His name. The perimeter of a square drawn on the outer face of the Sarsen Circle is 140.8 yards. The title, *Saviour, σωτηρ,* has a number value of 1408.

If the circumference of the inner face of the Sarsen Circle were measured in royal cubits it would be 177.7. The name, *Jesus of Nazareth, Ιησου Ναζωραιον,* has a value of 1777.

If the area contained within the outer face of the Sarsen Circle were computed with the ancient Roman pace, which was the equivalent of 2.4333 British feet, it would be 1480 Roman paces. The title, *Christ, Χριστος,* has a number value of 1480.

The radius of that outer face of the Sarsen Circle is .0800 furlongs. The title, *Lord,* has a value of 800, while the number

8 always symbolizes Jesus and the resurrection—a new beginning.

There are many more, but I do not wish to burden the reader. The above evidence is sufficiently overwhelming to prove the intent of the Architect.

The Sarsen Circle was made up of 30 upright stones, topped by 30 lintels. It was an ingenious construction, using mortise and tenon between uprights and lintels, and tongue-and-groove to join the lintels.

Lest we tend to overlook the marvelous engineering ability of the Architect, let us remember that those perfectly shaped and curved 7-ton lintels were tooled in the quarry 20 miles away, before being brought to the building site and lifted into place to form a perfect circle. The precision with which the lintels were tooled and placed, and the accuracy of the division of the circle into 30 equal parts, is awesome when we consider the time and circumstances under which Stonehenge was built.

The average of the widths of the uprights is 7.04 feet with intervals between of 3.52 feet. The number 704 is the gematria for *"holy place,"* $\alpha \gamma \iota o \nu \ \tau o \pi o \nu$. Surely, this was indeed a holy place, for it bore the name of the Saviour of mankind. The number 352 is the gematria for *"The Way,"* $\eta \ o \delta o \varsigma$—a title that Jesus applied to himself, for surely he was the way of life.

There were 30 of these uprights in the Sarsen Circle, thus 7.04 x 30 = 211.2. The prophecy concerning the birth of Jesus bears that number. *"A virgin shall conceive and bear a son, and shall call his name Emmanuel,"* הרה וילדת בן וקראת שמו עמנו אל העלמה, (Isaiah 7:14); the Hebrew letters add to 2112.

The interval between the uprights, when multiplied by 30 gives 105.6 (3.52 x 30 = 105.6). This is the number value of *"the heavenly man,"* $o \ \varepsilon \pi o v \rho \alpha v \iota o \varsigma$ (I Cor. 15:48). The number 1056 is also used regarding the purpose of his experience as a man. *"The joy of thy salvation,"* ששון ישעך, (Psalm 51:12) has a number equivalent of 1056. Also *"The cleft of the rock,"* הצור הנקרת, (Exodus 33:22) which hid Moses is a picture of Jesus as man's hiding place. It has the number value of 1056. Best of all

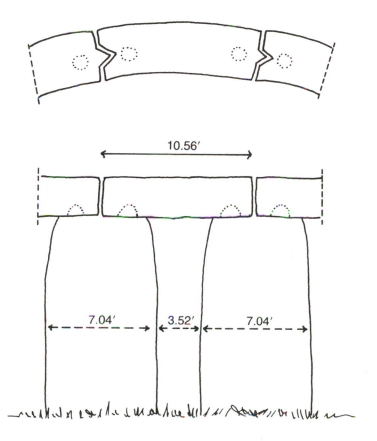

is the statement of Isaiah (19:20) *"He shall send them a saviour and a great one,"* ישלח להם מושיע ורב, which also has the number value of 1056.[1]

The importance of this number to the Sarsen Circle is

---

1 The actual number for this statement is 1057. By the rules of gematria, one or two numbers may be added or subtracted from a number to retain the meaning. This is called *colel,* in the Cabala.

emphasized by the beautiful lintels that were tooled and polished to form an interlocking circle—a circle level with gravity; for the height of the upright stones was carefully adjusted to compensate for the gentle slope of the ground. This perfect circle, lifted up from the earth upon the tops of the huge sarsen stones, contained 30 stones, each with a mean length of 10.56 feet (30 x 10.56 = 316.8).

The beauty and perfectness of that ring of lintels could only have been fully appreciated by viewing it from above. It is doubtful that the workmen who built it ever saw it from such a vantage point. If we were to measure it by another unit, the ancient Egyptian remen, it would measure 260. All who have studied the gematria of the Old Testament are aware of the significance of 26. It is the number equivalent of the holy unpronounceable name, יהוה, the Tetragrammaton, known to us as Jehovah, or Yahweh.

The number 26 in the gematria of the Old Testament is rich with meaning. The Hebrew word כבד means to be glorious, and has a number value of 26. The Hebrew word עלסלע, which means "on a rock," has the number value of 260. The phrase is referring to Jehovah, who is called a Rock throughout the Old Testament. Another use of the number 260 in the Old Testament is בקול יהוה אלהינ, "The Voice of the Lord our God." The Hebrew word כבד, meaning "great," also adds to 26.

In the New Testament the number 26 still sounds His praises, literally, for αινειν Θεον, "praise God," has a number equivalent of 260. "Holy ground," γη αγια, yields 26; and that circle of stones does indeed enclose holy ground, for the names of both the Father and the Son abound there.

The vertical thickness of those carefully tooled lintels was 2.36 feet, according to Petrie. The number is an interesting one. In Isaiah 60:15 the title, "Everlasting Majesty," לגאון עולם, is used, speaking of Jehovah. It has a number equivalent of 236. The prophet Jeremiah (Jer. 10:10) called him "The King Everlasting," מלך עולם, which also adds to 236.

Petrie actually carried the measurement out to four deci-

24

mal places—2.3666. If this were converted to megalithic yards, the measure would be .87 MY. In the Old Testament the exclamation *"I am Jehovah,"* אני יהוה, is used over and over again. It bears the number 87. In the New Testament *"the Lord,"* ο κυριος, is used throughout. It has the number equivalent of 87.

Each of those lintels had a mean length of 10.56 feet, precisely the length of the reed that Ezekiel saw in his vision of the temple. This was the height of the place in that temple called the *"Most Holy."*

This unit of measure—the reed— was a special one, given by God to the prophet Ezekiel in the year 573 B.C. That it should be used at Stonehenge roughly 1,400 years previously, speaks loudly that the building of Stonehenge was of divine design.

The length of this reed is recorded in Ezekiel 40:5: *"a measuring reed of six great cubits long, by the cubit and a hand breadth."*

Down through time, many units have been known as cubits, but the one given to Ezekiel was called the great cubit, which was a *"cubit and a hand breadth."* The cubit to which the hand breadth is added is one that was in common use in Ezekiel's day, known as the moderate cubit. The name distinguishes it from their longer cubit known to us as the royal cubit. The moderate cubit was their shorter one, equivalent to 18:14 British inches. In the Mishna it is defined as six hand breadths, or 144 barleycorns. The great cubit given to Ezekiel added one more hand breadth, or 3.02 more inches, making it equivalent to 21.12 British inches or 1.76 feet. Six of these great cubits made the reed of 10.56 feet or 126.72 inches.

The relationship of this God-given unit to Stonehenge is awesome.

The Sarsen Circle, complete with its ring of beautifully polished lintels had a maximum diameter of 1267.2 inches (the outer face of the circle), corresponding to the 126.72 inches of the reed. 12,672 inches is one fifth of a British mile.

Taking the radius of that outer face gives a length of 17.6 yards, corresponding to the length of the great cubit, 1.76 feet.

The length of the reed was 10.56 feet. This was not only the length of each of the sarsen lintels, it also relates to other measures of the Sarsen Circle. The diameter of the outer face of the circle is 105.6 feet, while the circumference of its mean is 105.6 yards.

Evidence reveals the probability that the builders of Stonehenge used the Great Cubit, for most of the circles were laid out in whole Great Cubits.

	Feet	Great Cubits
Circumference of mean of Sarsen Circle	316.8	180
Diameter of outer face of Sarsen Circle	105.6	60
Diameter of Bluestone Circle	79.2	45
Each lintel	10.56	6
Interval between Sarsen uprights	3.52	2
Long side of Station Stone rectangle	264	150
Diameter of Bluestone Horseshoe	39.6	22.5

That great cubit (1.76 feet, or 21.12 inches) and its multiple, the reed (10.56 feet) bear the name of Jesus.

1.76 x 2 = 3.52 *The Way,* η οδος, 352

1.76 x 5 = 8.8 *a child is born,* (Jesus) (Isaiah 9:6), 88

1.76 x 6 = 10.56 *The joy of thy salvation,* ששון ישע, (Psalm 51.12), 1056.

1.76 x 8 = 14.08 *Saviour,* σωτηρ, 1408

1.76 x 12 = 21.12 *Glory of the Lord,* δοξης του κυριου, 2112
A virgin shall conceive and bear a son, and shall call his name Emmanuel, שמו עמנו אל
העלמה הרה וילדת בן וקראת, 2112

1.76 x 13 = 22.88 *Christ the Lord,* Χριστος η Κυριος, 2288

1.76 x 15 = 26.4 *The Light* (Jesus), του φωτος, 2640

1.76 x 25 = 44 *Lamb* (picturing Jesus), טלה, 44

10.56 x 3 = 31.68   *Lord Jesus Christ, Κυριος Ιησους Χριστος,*
3168

The smoothly tooled ring of lintels that topped the Sarsen Circle were finished on both their inner and outer faces, indicating that both surfaces were significant measures. Just as the mean of that circle of lintels bore the number 26 (remens), the number for Jehovah, so the outer face bears the number for π (3.14159), for it has a circumference of 31.4159 reeds, or ten times π. No one has ever been able precisely to define π. It appears to be the number of infinity, for it will never come out even regardless of how many hundreds or even thousands of decimal places it is given. By its never ending nature, it aptly represents the eternal God. The *Almighty,* שדי, even bears the shortened version of π, 3.14 by its gematria of 314.

It becomes apparent that the Architect of Stonehenge used the π ratio. The outer polished surface of the lintels has a circumference of 31.4159 reeds, or 10 times π.

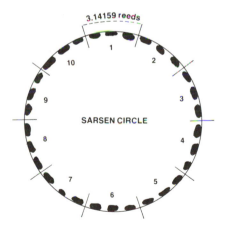

As if to emphasize the importance of that circle to the π value, and to the British mile, the area within its outer face is .000314159 of a square mile.

It has been suggested that the five trilithons each represent π. This is a visual association. Each of the free-standing sets are composed of two uprights topped by a lintel, forming the appearance of the Greek letter π. When this was suggested to me, I was asked to multiply 5 times π to see if the number was relevant. Thus 5 x 3.14159 = 15.70. In the second chapter of I Corinthians, the Apostle Paul expounded on the magnitude of the mind of God, showing how man, with his finite limitations cannot understand the infinite wisdom of God. He concluded by saying, *"For who hath known the mind of God!"* That entity, *"The mind of God,"* νουν Κυριου, has a number value of 1570, the same as 5π. That unfathomable mind speaks to us in many ways—through his word, through the universe, and through all creation. *"His glorious voice,"* הוד קולו, is, by gematria, the number 157. If Stonehenge is indeed of divine design, his glorious voice speaks to us through those ancient, lonely, silent, mute stones.

The function of those five trilithons was for the viewing of the rising and setting of the sun and moon at their extremes. They are the tallest stones of the structure. The uprights stood so close together that there was a minimum distance of less than a foot between them. To walk through the slot was obviously not the intent of the builder.

But if we were to walk amid those stones, we would find that only from specific vantage points can we view the horizon. All other views through their slots are blocked by the stones of the Sarsen Circle. The one thing each of these views of the horizon has in common is that, at the proper time of day, and the proper time of year, the sun or the moon can be seen on the horizon.

That horizon was provided by the bank that surrounded and formed the enclosure. That bank has been estimated by archaeologists to have been 6 feet high and 20 feet thick at its base— a rounded pile, dug from and thus forming the ditch which surrounds it. Today it is a gentle rising of the ground. The purpose of the bank, as well as providing a barrier defining the

The Moonrise Trilithon is awesome in its symmetry and workmanship. The view through the slot reveals the distant horizon.

limits of the enclosure, was to provide an artificial horizon for viewing the rising and setting of the sun and moon.

It is fitting that the diameter of the bank, at its crest, was 318 feet, for the word *sun, ηλιος,* has a number value of 318; while the radius was .0301 of a mile—301 being the number value of *moon, σεληνη.* The diameter of the bank at its crest was 30.1 reeds.

The light of the moon is the reflected light of the sun. They have the same source, thus:

318   *sun, ηλιος*
318   *He is my Rock,* הוא צורי, (Psalm 62:2)
301   *moon, σεληνη*
301   *He is the Rock,* הצור, (Deut. 32:4)

That bank which forms a horizon for viewing the sun and moon has a diameter of 318 feet, giving it a circumference of 999 feet. As we have seen, the number 9 represents a whole or complete concept or thing; in this case showing that all within this wall was a complete picture (just as 9 planets complete the solar system). The triplet of 9s is the concept raised to its highest order, that of divine arrangement (*"In the beginning God,"* 999, Genesis 1:1).

If, when converting the 318 feet in the diameter of the bank to reeds, we carried it out to two decimal places, it would be 30.11 reeds. Since these two numbers—318 and 301—represent the sun and moon, respectively, the two great lights, let's multiply by the number that represents the speed of the light that comes to us from the sun and the moon, 186—30.11 x 186 = 5600. It is a number that represents wholeness or everlastingness. The Hebrew word יום has a number value of 56, and is translated in the Old Testament by the English words *everlasting, forever, time, whole,* and *day.* How fitting that the circle of holes, immediately enclosed by the bank, named the Aubrey Circle, should number 56 holes around the circle. That circle, in fact, does prove to be a time line, like the numerals on the face of a giant clock.

In 1829 Godfrey Higgins, theorizing on the purpose of Stonehenge, suggested that the circles represented "astronomical cycles of antiquity."

I first became acquainted with Stonehenge in 1973. It was the Aubrey Circle that made me sit up and take notice. Why did it have a radius of 144 feet, and why were there 56 holes in the circumference? I knew that 144 was a Biblical number, as well as 7 and 8, which, when multiplied, produced 56. I had been a student of the chronology of man for many years, and had always worked with a time line on a flat plane. From many evidences in the Bible and elsewhere, it had seemed evident to me that the story of man was based in a cycle of 7,000 years. As I looked at the drawing of Stonehenge I pictured the Aubrey Circle as representing those 7,000 years, being divided into thousands by each increment of 8 holes. What would happen, I wondered, if the straight-line chronology were overlaid around this circle?

To accomplish this it was first necessary to find zero—the starting place on the circle.

The work of Professor Gerald Hawkins had proven that Stonehenge was aligned to the rising and setting of the sun and moon. It had been known, however, for many centuries previously, that the Heelstone was aligned to the sunrise at the summer solstice. It had, in fact, become a custom for people to gather at Stonehenge on the morning of summer solstice to watch this phenomenon. Professor Wm. Flinders Petrie, commenting on such activities in 1880 wrote, "The large numbers of people that keep up with much energy the custom of seeing the sunrise at midsummer, somewhat suggests that it is an old tradition; and hence that it has some weight, independent of the mere coincidence."

It was, of course, no "mere coincidence." Hawkins proved that with his computer. It was the planned orientation of the structure. This has led some archaeologists and researchers to conclude that the alignment of summer solstice sunrise was the designed axis of the monument. This alignment does provide an obvious intended line of sight that precisely bisects the circle. In fact, if the observer were to stand on the crest of the bank where this suggested axial line intersects, at the time that Stonehenge was built, he would see the full orb of the sun perfectly framed between archway 15-16 of the Sarsen Circle, the slot of the Great Central Trilithon (stones 55-56), the interval between Bluestones 31-49, the archway 1-30 of the Sarsen Circle, and perfectly fill the gap between the upright Slaughter Stone and its companion, as its brilliance appeared to rest atop the Heelstone, crowning it with its golden light. This alignment made Stonehenge the most precise solar observatory of the ancient world.

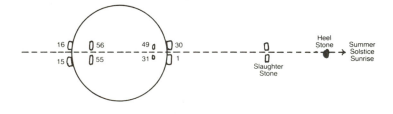

The azimuth of sunrise has gradually changed through the centuries because the sun slowly slips back along the ecliptic, causing its apparent position to move gradually to the east. The original alignment, however, is permanently fixed by the position of the Heelstone. Thus a line from the center of the Sarsen Circle to the center of the Heelstone is 51.85° from north, and will never change.

This suggested that if the Aubrey Circle were, in fact, a time line, the zero point would be the place where the axis intersects, facing sunrise. But in my search for the zero point, I also became aware of an astounding fact—the angle of sunrise to north at Stonehenge was the same exact angle as that of the face of the Great Pyramid, namely, 51.85°.

Assuming that the 360° of the Aubrey Circle could be a time line of 7,000 years, it was a simple matter of mathematics to determine that one year would equal .0514285°. I was off and running.

Hawkins had suggested that the Aubrey Circle provided a protractor for the measurement of azimuth, while the Bank provided an artificial horizon. Using this idea, Stonehenge could become a chronometer with the Aubrey Circle as the date line: one circuit of its circumference could represent a period of 7,000 years relative to man's history. The azimuths, or the points at which each alignment intersects the Aubrey Circle would become date points. According to Bible chronologers, this span of 7,000 years is called a *day*. It is the Hebrew word יום which has a number value of 56, corresponding to the 56 holes of the Aubrey Circle.

With these evidences as the key, I attempted the correlation of all the solar and lunar alignments that Hawkins found from his computer. The correspondencies were astounding! They all related to important Biblical dates and events.

Next I attempted the correlation of all the stone alignments with the chronology of man. They all worked. That ancient structure had been designed by someone with a knowledge of the future, for it told the whole history of man's relationship with his Creator.

Still wondering if this was indeed of the original design, I decided to put the theory to a test. I moved the zero point to other places on the Aubrey Circle and attempted to fit it into the chronology of man. Nothing worked! After many attempts, I had to be satisfied with the evidence that the Aubrey Circle was indeed a time line and that the summer solstice sunrise marked the zero point of the circle.

A detailed, in-depth description of each alignment and its relationship to the history of man is available in *Stonehenge...a closer look,*[1] and is too lengthy to repeat here. However, one prominent feature of that study is appropriate for the purpose of this current work. It is the alignment of the equinox moon.

Professor Hawkins has shown that the equinox moon had been marked by a number of alignments. The equinox is the midpoint between the two extremes of the sun, when night and day become of equal length. The equinox moon is the full moon nearest the equinox. In the spring it is the Passover moon. One of these alignments was stone number 94 (one of the Station Stones) to the Heelstone. A line drawn parallel to this that would pass through the Sarsen Center would intersect the Aubrey Circle (the date line) in the spring of 3473 B.C. and A.D. 33.

On the afternoon of April 3, 33 A.D., Jesus hung upon a cross atop Golgotha's hill. April 3 of that year was the day of Passover. At 3:00 in the afternoon the Passover lambs were to be slain. At 3:00 that very afternoon the Lamb of God died on the cross. At 3:06 Greenwich time (Stonehenge time) that full

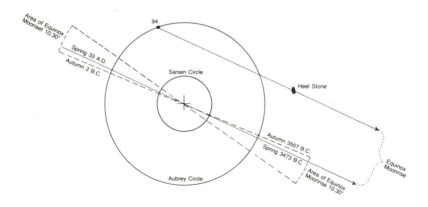

---

1 Bonnie Gaunt, *Stonehenge...a closer look,* Bonnie Gaunt, 510 Golf Avenue, Jackson, Michigan 49203, U.S.A., 1979, $10.00.

moon eclipsed. As the moon arose over Jerusalem that awful night, it was still eclipsed for seventeen minutes.

The Architect of Stonehenge had monumentalized in stone, for all time, and for all to see, the importance of the death of Jesus, the date of the event, and its occurrence on the afternoon of Passover (equinox) moonrise.

The other point of intersection of this Passover moon alignment represents the spring of 3473 B.C. Did anything of importance happen then? Yes! Just as the A.D. 33 date showed Jesus at the age of $33^1/_2$, so the other end of the alignment shows Enoch at the age of $33^1/_2$. Students of Scripture often see a correlation between the life of Enoch and the life of Jesus. The first becomes an illustration of the second.

This alignment of the Passover moon, intersecting the Aubrey Circle at A.D. 33 is an important pivotal point in the value of this work, and I will return to it subsequently; however, it is necessary at this time to deal with other important considerations of Stonehenge, to lay a proper foundation for understanding.

We saw the Passover moon alignment as originating with Station Stone 94. Further description of the Station Stones and their function is appropriate here.

Approximately in the line of the circumference of the 56 holes of the Aubrey Circle were four unhewn boulders that have since been called Station Stones. These four stones form the corners of a rectangle. They have been numbered by Petrie, 91, 92, 93 and 94, merely for identification. Only 91 and 93 remain today. Stones 91 and 92 are parallel with the axis and therefore are aligned to the summer solstice sunrise, as are their partners, stones 93 and 94. These are the short side of the rectangle. The long sides align with the moon nearest the solstice. The two stones which remain today, 93 and 91, the diagonal of the rectangle, are also aligned to the moon.

The Architect of Stonehenge chose the one spot in the northern hemisphere where the sun and moon alignments would form a rectangle. Men have attempted to build replicas and models of Stonehenge elsewhere in the world, but if they wanted to make the station stones align with the sun and moon, they would have various shaped parallelograms. It will only form a rectangle at one location on earth; for its counterpart in the southern hemisphere is in the ocean.

This unique rectangle does, among other things, serve as a standard for linear measure. Its long side measured 264 feet, which is the 20th part of a mile. It could be called a *sign,* or that which points to something of importance. I believe it is beyond

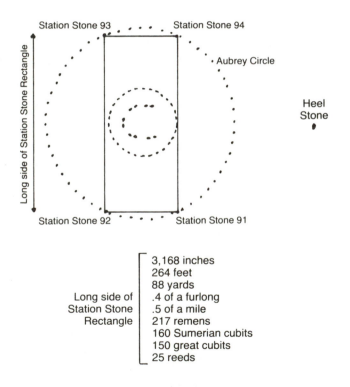

Station Stone 93	Station Stone 94

Aubrey Circle

Heel
Stone

Long side of Station Stone Rectangle

Station Stone 92 Station Stone 91

Long side of
Station Stone
Rectangle
3,168 inches
264 feet
88 yards
.4 of a furlong
.5 of a mile
217 remens
160 Sumerian cubits
150 great cubits
25 reeds

36

coincidence that the number 264 in the gematria of the New Testament has the same meaning. The Greek word σημεια, 264, is translated by the English word *signs* in Acts 2:19. The same Greek word is translated *wonders* and *miracles* in the book of Revelation. The word *truth* in Greek is αληθειας and has a number equivalent of 264.

The name Jesus is also planted there. In John 1:7 he is called *"the Light,"* του φωτος, 2640. In Romans 8:3 his purpose as man's redeemer is referred to when it says he came *"in the likeness of sinful flesh,"* εν ομοιωματι σαρκος αμαρτιας, 2640. And James 5:8 tells of *"the coming of the Lord,"* η παρουσια του Κυριου, 2640.

If we take this measure in inches it would be 3168, the number for the name Lord Jesus Christ. In yards it would be 88, the number used in the prophecy of Isaiah 9:6 referring to the birth of Jesus—*"a child is born,"* ילד ילד, 88.

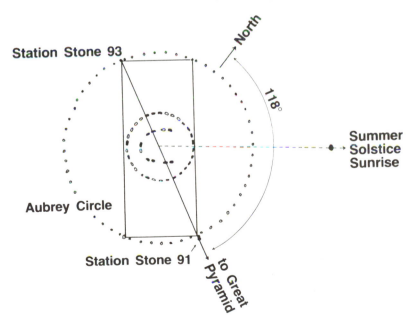

This long side of the Station Stone Rectangle appears to serve as a standard for linear units. The fact that its length of 264 feet reveals its use as a *sign* and a *wonder,* takes on importance of fantastic proportion. It is indeed a sign pointing to the greatest wonder of the world, the Great Pyramid.

The diagonal of that rectangle, from stones 93 to 91 is the alignment of the moonrise *high* nearest the summer solstice. However, if you were to walk from stone 93 to stone 91, and kept on walking in that precise direction around the world, you would bump into the Great Pyramid. In other words, the exact azimuth from Station Stone 93 to Station Stone 91 is, in fact, the arc of a great circle that passes through both Stonehenge and the Great Pyramid—two wonders of the ancient world. The diagonal of that remarkable rectangle becomes a *sign,* pointing the way to the Great Pyramid.

That diagonal between Station Stones 93 and 91 measures 96 yards. The number 96 is the gematria for *"The secret of the Lord,"* סוד יהוה, (Psalm 25:14). Surely it points to the most amazing secret ever given to man—the Great Pyramid.

The front, or north face of the Great Pyramid.

Photo by Todd Alexander

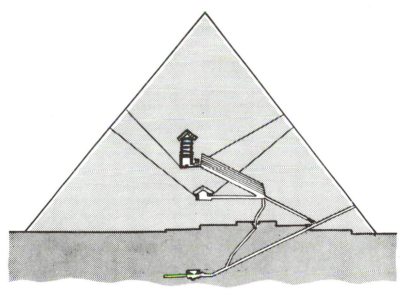

The vertical meridian section of the Great Pyramid, showing its passage and chamber system.

39

Photo by Todd Alexander

Photo by Todd Alexander

The Great Pyramid stands as a silent sentinel, as more than 1,500,000 mornings and evenings cast their shadows over the sands of the Nile delta.

3

Pyramid Secrets

The Station Stone rectangle with its diagonal pointing precisely to the Great Pyramid appears to be a key that could unlock a great secret.

The 96 yards of the Station Stone rectangle not only points to *"The secret of the Lord,"* it also, by gematria, points to *"a kingdom,"* מלכו, 96. Measuring it in feet would give 288, and *"the kingdom of heaven,"* βασιλεια των ουρανων, has the number value of 288.

Palmoni, the Numberer of Secrets, who spoke to Daniel, does, by his very name, tell us that secrets are locked up in numbers. The Great Pyramid has been one of those secrets. It has kept its silent vigil over the Nile delta for over 4,000 years, and is still considered to be one of the greatest mysteries ever known to man.

Its base covers 13 acres, the perimeter of which, at rock level, measures 3041.28 feet. If this measure were converted to reeds it would be 288, the same as the number of feet in the diagonal of the Station Stone rectangle—the *sign* pointing to the Great Pyramid.

Each side of the Great Pyramid at its rock level measures 72 reeds. The Hebrew word for *secret* or *in secret,* is בסוד, which bears the number 72. There has never been a more profound secret than the Great Pyramid. Its four sides speak to us the words *secret, secret, secret, secret!* And the darkness that lies within has hidden its secrets for over 4,000 years.

The number 72 resolves to 9, showing the completeness, or

41

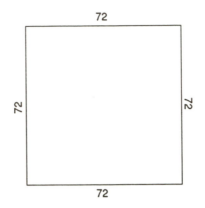

Each side, 72 — *Secret,* בסוד, 72
Perimeter, 288 — Base perimeter of Pyramid, 288 reeds.

wholeness, of its message—a message preserved in stone. How fitting that the Greek word τοπος, meaning *stone,* should bear the number 720; or that η αληθεια, *the truth,* should also give the number 72.

Is it coincidence that ο εκλεκτος, *"The Chosen One,"* (meaning Jesus Christ) has a number value of 720? What does Jesus Christ have to do with the Great Pyramid or its secrets?

At Stonehenge we saw how the Aubrey Circle served as a date line, measuring the history of man. Those who have studied the measurements of the Great Pyramid believe that its passage system is a similar time line; the formula being one Pyramid inch[1] equals one year.

Measuring up the First Ascending Passage, by this formula, would bring us to the date A.D. 33 at the juncture of the passage system as shown in the illustration below. Jesus died on April 3, 33 A.D.

---

1 The Pyramid inch was a unit of measure in the structural design of the Great Pyramid. It is described as 1 Pyramid inch equals 1.00106 British inches, or 1 British inch equals .99894 of a Pyramid inch.

PYRAMID SECRETS

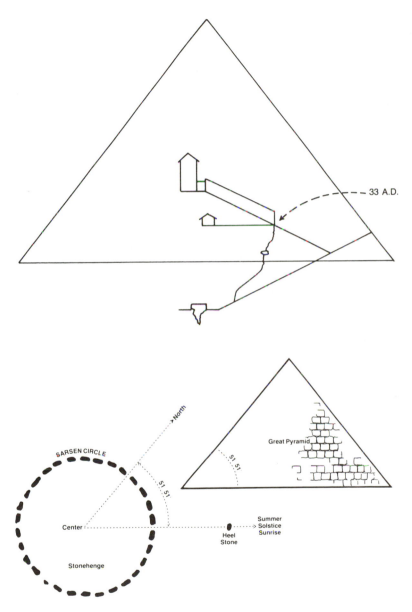

- - - 33 A.D.

SARSEN CIRCLE

North

Great Pyramid

51 51'

51 51'

Center

Heel
Stone

Summer
Solstice
Sunrise

Stonehenge

43

Stonehenge was built on the only spot in the northern hemisphere where the azimuth of summer solstice sunrise formed an angle of 51.85° from north. It is the same as the famous Pyramid angle. Thus the angle of the Great Pyramid fits precisely into the angle of sunrise-to-north at Stonehenge.

It seemed only logical to overlay a scale drawing of the Great Pyramid on a drawing of Stonehenge to the same scale. The results were astounding! Line up a straight-edge with the socket level base of the Great Pyramid, and raise it to the level of the intersection of the passage that is said to mark the date A.D. 33. The other end of the straight edge will exactly intersect the Aubrey Circle at the date point of A.D. 33. It will even form a 33° angle with the alignment of the Passover moon at Stonehenge.

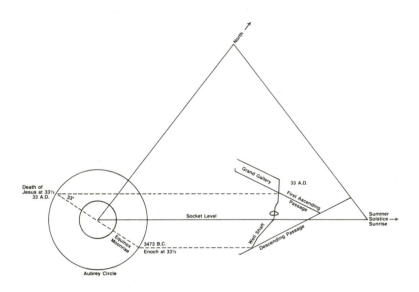

Lower the straight edge to the point of intersection of the descending passage with the bottom of the Well. The other end of the straight edge will intersect the Aubrey Circle at precisely the date 3473 B.C., when Enoch was 33^1/$_2$ years old.

Both ends of the Passover moon alignment at Stonehenge perfectly correspond to the two ends of the Well at the Great Pyramid.

But why the Well? Does the Well relate to the Passover moon in any way? Does it relate to Jesus Christ?

The noted author and researcher, Morton Edgar, concluded that the passage and chamber system of the Great Pyramid had not only time measurement, but symbolic meaning as well. Similar research has been done, and similar conclusions reached by many authors. Adam Rutherford, of the Institute of Pyramidology, in Herfordshire, England, not only gave us accurate measurement of the passages and chambers, he also suggested their obvious symbolic meaning.

Briefly stated, the suggested symbol was that the Descending Passage represented mankind's downward course leading to death, because of the disobedience of Adam. The First Ascending Passage would represent a way to life through the keeping of the Mosaic Law. But that law, instead of giving life through the keeping of it, brought death through the breaking of it. Thus the three solid granite plugs that completely fill the lower end of the First Ascending Passage prevent any from traversing the passage upward.

Near the end of that Law age, Jesus was born. At the age of 33^1/$_2$ he was put to death on the cross, but arose again to provide life for all mankind. Thus the Well illustrates that way of life through Jesus Christ.

The Passage to the Queen's Chamber represents the way to everlasting life in the earthly portion of Christ's Millennial Kingdom; while the Grand Gallery's upward passage pictures the walk and development of the Christian toward a heavenly home, pictured by the King's Chamber.

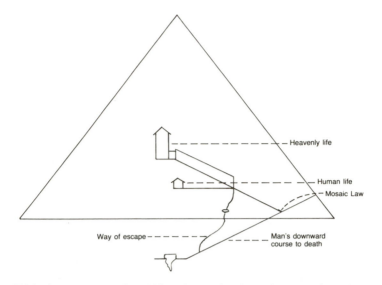

This is an over-simplification of a lengthy and involved subject that some authors have used two, three, and even four volumes to describe. But I did not want the reader to lose sight of the beautiful correlation between the Great Pyramid and Stonehenge, as shown by the Well and the Passover moon alignment. The correspondence is so remarkable that, considering the time and space that separates the construction of these two monuments, it is certanly worthy of our sincere consideration.

When the Apostle Paul said *"Christ, our Passover, is sacrificed for us,"* (I Cor. 5:7), he was telling us that Jesus Christ was taking the place of the typical Passover lamb. He became the fulfillment of the type—the real event to which the type had pointed. Both the Passover moon alignment at Stonehenge and the Well of the Great Pyramid illustrate that event. The fact that they perfectly correspond geometrically, though more than 2,300 miles apart, leaves no room for coincidence. It was the intended design of the Architect.

"Christ our passover," πασχα ημων Χριστος, has the

number value of 3260. It is also interesting that 326 is the number value of Γεθσημανι, Gethsemane, for while he prayed that night in Gethsemane, under the Passover full moon, he knew that he would soon be slain as the Passover Lamb.

A circle with a diameter of 326 has a circumference of 1024, which, when defined as a square, would have sides of 256. How fitting that 256 is the gematria for ""*Thy kingdom is an everlasting kingdom and thy dominion throughout all generations,*" (Psalm 145:13). By fulfilling the purpose of the Passover Lamb, he not only purchased life for mankind, but also an everlasting kingdom.

The Well in the Great Pyramid serves as an illustration of the death and resurrection of Jesus. Down in the midst of the Well is a secret cave, a natural grotto in the rock. This small cavern was in the natural rock before the Pyramid was built above it. It holds a secret that very few men have ever seen.

In 1966, August Tornquist and Frank Shallieu, two American researchers, were photographing the interior of the Great Pyramid. After the dangerous climb up the steep and narrow Well shaft, they entered the dark Grotto. With flashlights and candles, they broke the darkness and began an exploration of the cavern, photographing it from many angles.

Back in the United States again, they were giving a slide presentation of the Great Pyramid, and, upon showing a picture of the Grotto, a woman in the audience exclaimed, "I see a lamb's head." They examined the photo more carefully; yes, there did indeed appear to be a lamb's head protruding from the side wall of the Grotto.

In February of 1978, August Tornquist returned to the Great Pyramid with a young assistant, Todd Alexander, again to take photos of the passages and chamber system. They climbed the difficult Well shaft and into the Grotto—this time looking for the lamb's head.

They found the head, a natural stone formation about 36 inches tall, protruding about 18 inches from the wall of the Grotto.

Photos by Todd Alexander

Todd Alexander and August Tornquist, with lamb's head in the Grotto.

The Grotto is a natural cave in the rock, that existed long before the Great Pyramid was built above it. The lamb's head is part of that natural formation. There is no evidence of tooling. In the book of Revelation we are told of *"The Lamb slain from the foundation of the world,"* (13:8). That Lamb was Jesus, who was put to death at the very hour, on Nisan 14, that the Passover lambs were being slain. He was the great Passover Lamb, and his role as that Lamb was part of God's plan from before the foundation of the world.

The existence of the lamb's head in the Grotto is a secret that the Great Pyramid has held for over 4,000 years; but it was there from time unknown.

The secrets of the Great Pyramid are hidden in number. Palmoni, the Numberer of Secrets, left his number there. Palmoni, פלמוני, bears the number 216; a number planted in the universe. The diameter of our moon is 2,160 miles, and 2,160 is the number of years in each division of the Zodiac. The number signifies power and greatness, for the Hebrew word גבורה, is translated *power,* and *mighty* in the Old Testament scriptures, and it bears the number 216. It is also the number for *lion,* אריה, which we have called the king of beasts, but both Old and New Testaments call Jesus the *"Lion of the tribe of Judah."* The number 2160 takes on more comprehensive proportions when we realize it is the number equivalent for *"Kingdom of the Father,"* βασιλεια των πατρος, (Matt. 13:43).

Palmoni left his number in both the base and the topstone of the Great Pyramid. Three sides of the rock level base measures 216 reeds; the unit given by God to Ezekiel. In the New Testament the topstone of the Great Pyramid is used metaphorically of Jesus, and he is called *"The stone which the builders rejected,"* λιθον ον απεδοκιμασαν οι οικοδο-μουντες, (Matt. 21:42), which has the number value of 2160. The topstone was literally rejected because it was never lifted into place on the Pyramid.

216 is a number which connects the Great Pyramid with the universe, with our solar system, with Jesus Christ, and with the *"Kingdom of the Father."* The number resolves to 9, showing its wholeness and perfection. Palmoni, whoever he is, bears a beautiful number. He is the Wonderful Numberer, the Numberer of Secrets. His name is *secret* (72), *secret* (72), *secret* (72)— 3 x 72 = 216.

The bedrock upon which the Great Pyramid is built rises beneath the interior, making it possible for the secret Grotto to be above the level of the base of the structure. The perimeter of the base rests on a platform placed upon this bedrock. The perimeter of the Great Pyramid at this level of its bedrock is 3041 feet.

When the rock level base perimeter is measured with the

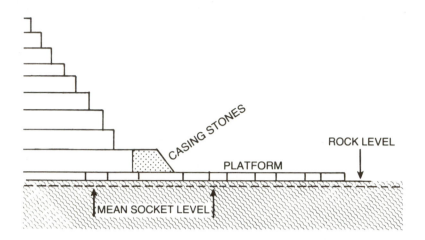

reed, its numbers begin revealing its secrets. We saw how one side, being 72 reeds, tells us it is secret, but it also tells us it is *truth, η αληθεια, 72.*

Two sides measure 144 reeds. It is the number for *everlasting,* קדם, 144, and the number for *divine nature, θειον,* 144. It is the number signifying divine authority and power; for the proclamation *"The Lord said unto my Lord, sit thou on my right hand until I make thine enemies thy footstool,"* (Acts 2:34), adds to 14400.

In the book of Revelation, John described a marvelous scene that was given to him in vision. He told of a Lamb standing on Mount Zion, and with him were 144,000 faithful believers, the elect of God. The number 1440 is the gematria for *believers, πιστων;* it is also the number value for "elect of God," *εκλογην του Θεου.* "The elect," *η εκλογη,* bears the number 144.

Four sides of this marvelous structure at its rock base measures 288 reeds. Aside from it being twice 144, its significance is revealed in its use in the scriptures. *"Kingdom of heaven," βασιλεια των ουρανων,* gives a number equivalent of 2880. Referring to Jesus as the King in that kingdom, the prophet Zechariah said that *"He shall be a priest on his throne,"* והיה כהן על כסאו, which adds to 288. Yes, the base of the Great Pyramid tells us of a glorious kingdom of God and of its King, Jesus Christ. It also relates to the Aubrey Circle at Stonehenge, whose diameter is 288 feet. The gematria for Jesus Christ, *Ιησους Χριστος,* is 2368. Multiply the digits, 2 x 3 x 6 x 8 = 288.

Thus the reed—the unit of measure given to Ezekiel—reveals some of the secrets, locked in number, in the Great Pyramid. The reed was made of 6 great cubits. Let's try measuring the rock level base of the Great Pyramid using the great cubit.

One side would measure 432 great cubits. The radius of the sun is 432,000 miles, and the number 432 is a number that relates to the entire universe in Revelation 4:11 by the Greek word *παντα, "all things."* The statement reads, *"Thou hast created all things, and for thy pleasure they are and were created."* In Colossians 3:11 this word is used again in stating that Christ is *"all things."* In Revelation 21:5 we have been given the beautiful promise that God would make *"all things"* new—referring to the time when his kingdom is complete. The number 432 resolves to 9, showing its wholeness and perfection.

That the foundation of the Great Pyramid bears the number 432 is most appropriate, for the word *foundation, καταβολη,* has the number value of 432, as does *σημειον μεγα, "a great wonder"* (sign). Surely the Great Pyramid, the greatest wonder in the world, is the *sign* that Isaiah spoke of:

> *In that day shall there be an altar to the Lord in the midst of the land of Egypt, and a pillar at the border thereof to the Lord. And it shall be for a sign and for a witness...*(Isaiah 19:19-20).

Two sides of the base of the Great Pyramid would thus

51

measure 864 great cubits, twice 432. The diameter of the sun is 864,000 miles. The number 864 is the value of *"cornerstone,"* γωνια, meaning the topstone of the Pyramid. That topstone, which was never placed, not only represents Jesus Christ, but it also represents the sun, from which flows light and life. *Life,* ζωην, bears the number 864. The dwelling place of God to which Lucifer aspired, *"The sides of the north,"* bears the number 864, as does *"Holy of holies,"* the compartment in the Tabernacle and in Ezekiel's temple that represents God's dwelling place. As if to emphasize the importance of this number, the *"Holy of holies,"* has the number value of 864 both in the Old Testament (Hebrew), and in the New Testament (Greek). Thus αγιων and קדש הקדשים both, by gematria, are 864.

The New Jerusalem, picturing the kingdom, is shown as coming down from God out of heaven in Revelation 3:12. *Jerusalem, Ιερουσαλημ,* bears the number 864. In that kingdom *"He shall reign,"* βασιλευσει, 864; and those who reign with him are called *"Saints,"* αγιων, 864. And *God, Θεων,* 864, will be all in all! Then will be the time that the prophet Micah spoke of, when will go forth *"the word of the Lord from Jerusalem,"* ודבר יהוה מירושלם, 864—the New Jerusalem.

The New Jerusalem, described in Revelation, has a sum of 864,000,000 square furlongs, the sum of the square of its six sides.

The number 864 resolves to 9, showing the wholeness and perfection of God's plan for the redemption of man and the ultimate restoration to sonship in His glorious kingdom. Thus the two sides of the Great Pyramid's base tell the wonderful story by the unlocking of the number 864.

Three sides of the base at rock level measure 1,296 great cubits, and the beauty of the story of God's glorious kingdom continues to unfold: *"My salvation from generation to generation,"* ישועתי לדור דורים, (Isaiah 51:8) bears the number 1296.

All four sides of the base of the Great Pyramid (its perimeter) measures 1,728 great cubits. *Holy Jerusalem, αγιων Ιερουσαλημ,* (Rev. 21:10) has the number value of 1728—the completed picture. Thus the numbers of the base of the Pyramid reveal *"the deep and secret things,"* עמיקתא ומסתרתא, 1728 (Daniel 2:22). Not only does it reveal the secret, it proclaims it to all mankind—*proclaim,* κηρυσσω, 1728.

It is interesting to note that the radius of the Aubrey Circle at Stonehenge measures 1728 inches, or 144 feet; and we saw how two sides of the base of the Great Pyramid measured 144 reeds. The Station Stone rectangle at Stonehenge has a perimeter of .144 of a mile, and the length of one side of the Great Pyramid measures .144 of a mile. In other words, if we straightened out the Station Stone rectangle to make a straight measuring line, it would exactly measure one side of the Great Pyramid at its rock level.

Two sides would then be .288 of a mile, three sides would be .432 of a mile, and the perimeter would be .576 of a mile. The Great Pyramid, the *sign,* מופתים, 576, and wonder in the land of Egypt reveals its secret *treasures,* מסכנות, 576. It is telling us *"In God is my salvation,"* (Psalm 62:7), על אלהים ישעי, 576. It speaks to us of *"His holy habitation,"* מעון קדשו, 576, which is the New Jerusalem. By the passage and chamber system it is telling us the *gospel,* ευαγγελιον, 576, of salvation for mankind. Its Well pictures the way of *life,* πνευμα, 576, through Jesus Christ.

The base platform of the Great Pyramid, resting on the natural bedrock foundation thus appears to have a positive identification with the gospel of salvation through Jesus Christ; but in doing this, it appears also to be a standard for the British mile, the megalithic mile, and the great cubit. Amazingly, when measured by the megalithic mile, one side would be .0528 MMi, corresponding to the number of feet in the British mile, 5280. However, when measuring all four sides by the megalithic mile, it will be .2112 MMi, corresponding to the number of inches in the great cubit, 21.12 .

528 is the number of *royalty,* βασιλειος. It is also *"The key,"* מפתח, 528, to the house of God (Isaiah 22:22). The number 2112 is the gematria for the *"glory of the Lord,"* δοξης του

Κυριου, (II Thes. 2:14), as well as being the number equivalent of *"A virgin shall conceive and bear a son and shall call his name Emmanuel,"* (Isaiah 7:14).

At each of the four corners of the Great Pyramid there are sockets that have been sunk into the bedrock. In the Old Testament, the book of Job contains some profound statements regarding the beginning of things. God asked Job:

> *Where wast thou when I laid the foundations of the earth? Declare if thou hast understanding. Who laid the measures thereof, if thou knowest? Or who hath stretched the measuring line upon it? Upon what are her foundation-pillars made to sink? Or who laid the cornerstone?* (Job 38:6).

It sounds more like a description of the Great Pyramid than of the earth. And very probably a simile was intended.[1] The Great Pyramid does indeed have foundation-pillars that are sunk beneath its four base corners; and it does have a magnificent cornerstone—a topstone that has never been placed upon its summit platform, but would have been about 48 feet wide and about 30 feet high. Some even suggest it was covered with gold.

Measuring the Great Pyramid to the full intended width on these corner sockets, each side would be 9131.05 Pyramid inches, or 365.242 Pyramid cubits.[2] The full circuit of its base perimeter would be 36524.2 Pyramid inches. This relates to earth's orbit around the sun, which takes 365.242 days. The square base of the Great Pyramid does, in fact, relate to its glorious topstone in the same manner that the earth relates to the sun. Its square base is to its height, from socket level to

---

1   The simile of the foundations of the earth and the Great Pyramid is discussed in depth in *The Stones Cry Out,* 1991, pp. 85-112, Bonnie Gaunt, 510 Golf Avenue, Jackson, Michigan 49203, U.S.A., $7.00.

2   The Pyramid cubit is 25 Pyramid inches.

apex, exactly as a circle is to its radius. Thus the 36524.2 Pyramid inches of its perimeter is as one orbit of the earth around the sun.

The mean distance from earth to the sun is rounded to 93 million miles, making the mean diameter of its orbit 186 million miles.

We saw how the height of the Great Pyramid, from its socket level to its glorious topstone, would have been 485 feet, and 485 is the gematria for *"There is no Rock like our God,"* ואין צור כאלהינו (II Samuel 2:2). That he should be called a Rock in this statement whose number value is the same as the height of the Great Pyramid is most significant, for that Pyramid is the greatest pile of rocks known to man.

It is also beautiful to note that 485 is the gematria for *"The sanctuary of God,"* מקדשי אל (Psalm 73:17), which seems to speak of this magnificent structure that presents His complete plan for the salvation of man through Jesus Christ.

That beautiful topstone, if it had been placed on the summit of the completed Pyramid, would have been glorious. It represents the sun, which in turn, represents God. How fitting that 485 is also the number value of *"The Lord shall be unto you an everlasting light,"* והיהלך יהוה לאור עולם (Isaiah 60:19).

The diameter of the sun is 864,000 miles, and it is most fitting that the solar number would be used for the gematria of that glorious topstone of the Pyramid—$\gamma\omega\nu\iota\alpha$, 864.

With this topstone picturing the sun, the base perimeter of the entire structure, 36524.2 Pyramid inches, beautifully represents earth's orbit around the sun, which has a mean diameter of 186 million miles—the number that represents the speed at which light comes to us from the sun. The base of the Pyramid rests on the natural bedrock, while the four corner sockets were sunk into the bedrock. 99% of the bedrock of earth's crust is composed of 12 elements. Their atomic numbers (the number of protons in the nucleus of each) total 186.

Oxygen	8
Silicon	14
Aluminum	13
Iron	26
Calcium	20
Sodium	11
Potassium	19
Magnesium	12
Titanium	22
Phosphorus	15
Hydrogen	1
Manganese	25
	186

The Creator is spoken of in scripture as the personification of light, as well as of rock. David wrote *"Jehovah is my Rock,"* יהוה סלע, 186; and Moses wrote it in song when he said *"He is the Rock, His work is perfect,"* (Deut. 32:4). By the phrase, *"His work,"* פעלו, Moses was obviously referring to the work of the creation of the world. In Hebrew it adds to 186. In Isaiah 64:4 the Hebrew word מעולם is used with reference to the beginning of the world. Its number value is 186.

The bedrock into which the four corner sockets were sunk bears the number 186. The four foundation-pillars of which God spoke to Job would therefore be 4 x 186 = 744, representing one circuit of the base perimeter of the Great Pyramid. If this were a circle, as is represented by the mean orbit of earth around the sun, the diameter of the circle would be 236.8, the number equivalent of Jesus Christ, Ιησους Χριστος, 2368.

That the number 744 relates to the foundation of the Great Pyramid is alluded to in the description of the laying of the foundation of the temple; they *"laid the foundation of the house,"* יהב אש די בית, 744 (Ezra 30:19).

This relationship of the earth to the sun, as is represented by the Pyramid's base to its topstone, would also apply to the moon, since it also orbits the sun along with the earth. How appropriate that the Genesis account of creation speaks of the making of *"two great lights,"* המאורת הגדלים, 744, the sun and the moon.

The sun has a diameter of 864,000 miles and is represented by the topstone which, by gematria, bears the number 864, *γωνια, cornerstone.*

The base perimeter of the Great Pyramid at its socket level measures 761.73 feet on each side. Rounded to 762 it is the number of *"The Rock of our salvation,"* לצור ישענו (Psalm 95:1). Multiplied by 4 it gives the base perimeter of 3048 feet, which is the gematria for *"the Saviour of the world,"* ο σωτηρ του κοσμου, 3048 (John 4:42).

The height of the Great Pyramid, from its socket level to the top of its glorious topstone would have measured 485 feet. If that measure were taken as one side of a square, the perimeter would be 1940 feet. This represents the entire structure and all that it contains within. The number 1940 is the gematria for *"eternal inheritance,"* αιωνιου κληρονομιας, (Heb. 9:15). It is a most appropriate name for the complete structure; for its passages and chambers beautifully illustrate the plan of God for the eternal salvation of man and his inheritance of life through Jesus Christ. *"Jesus and the resurrection,"* Iησουν και την ανασταστιν, (Acts. 17:18) has a number value of 1940, and this is what the symbolism of the Great Pyramid is all about. Its Well represents the only way to life, through the death and resurrection of Jesus Christ; and *"the way,"* οδον, has a number value of 194. The ultimate attainment, represented by the two upper chambers, is *righteousness,* צדק, 194.

Some may say, was not the Great Pyramid just the tomb of the ancient Pharaoh, Khufu? It is interesting how myths prevail even when evidences disproving them are made known. Egyptologist W. Marsham Adams, in *House of the Hidden Places,* reasoned:

That its various features are meaningless, or the mere result of caprice, is a suggestion to which the forethought and lavishness of calculation displayed in every detail unmistakably gives the lie. Nor again can we maintain that they are necessary for the purposes of an ordinary tomb.... For, they are not to be found in other pyramids which were used for that purpose.

Historians are nearly all in agreement that no one was ever buried there. And as for Khufu, or Cheops, as he was also called, his tomb has been found nearby. Egyptologists inform us that he was buried in an elaborately-cut sepulcher about a thousand feet from the Great Pyramid.

The researcher and author, Joseph A. Seiss, in his wonderful treatise on the Great Pyramid which he entitled *Miracle in Stone,*[1] made this summation regarding the historians' view of the tomb theory.

Helfricus (1565) and Baumgarten (1594) considered the Great Pyramid a tomb, but held that no one was ever buried in it. Pietro Della Valle (1616), Thevenot (1655), and Maillet (1692), give it the common belief that no one ever was therein entombed. Shaw (1721) denies that it ever was a tomb or ever was intended to be one. Mr. St. John does not consider the coffer a sarcophagus at all, and thinks the Great Pyramid never was, and never was meant to be a tomb.

The truth is that the tomb theory does not fit the facts, the traditions, or any knowledge that we have on the subject. It is wholly borrowed from the numerous later pyramids, ambitiously and ignorantly copied after it, which *were* intended and used for royal sepulchres, but with which the Great Pyramid has nothing in

Joseph A. Seiss, *Miracle in Stone,* The Castle Press, Philadelphia, 1877, p. 183.

common, save locality and general shape. In all the examination to which it has been subjected, whether in ancient or modern times, and in all the historic fragments concerning it, there is nothing whatever to give or to bear out the idea that its intention was that of a royal sepulchral monument, or that can legitimately raise the tomb theory any higher than a possible, but very improbable *supposition.*

The "numerous later pyramids" to which Seiss made reference are about thirty-eight in all, and they dot the western side of the Nile along the edge of the great Sahara Desert. They are all smaller and inferior in quality and workmanship to the Great Pyramid. They all, with the exception of the Great Pyramid, have one thing in common: they have no upper passages and chambers.

Why would all the other pyramids have only descending passages leading to underground burial chambers, if they were copied after the design of the Great Pyramid?

In the year A.D. 820, the Caliph Al Mamoun, the ruler in Baghdad, employed a vast number of architects, engineers and stone masons in the hope of entering the Great Pyramid and looting its treasures. The Caliph was particularly interested in celestial maps that were rumored to be there, for he was an accomplished astronomer. His interest in astronomy thus led him to the Great Pyramid and an attempt to explore its secret interior.

For many days his men searched the north face for the secret entrance that had been sealed and hidden. No trace of it could be found. Having heard that its entrance was on the north face, and hence that its passage system originated there, he decided to force his way in through the solid limestone.

His men soon found that hammer and chisel were inadequate—they could not penetrate the strength of those huge limestone blocks. So a more scientific method was employed. They built fires close to the limestone blocks, and when they became red hot, the workmen would pour cold vinegar over them until they cracked. The fragmented stones were then knocked loose by the use of battering rams.

Al Mamoun's forced entrance.

Photo by Todd Alexander

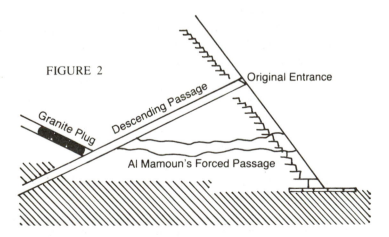

FIGURE 2

Granite Plug

Descending Passage

Original Entrance

Al Mamoun's Forced Passage

After tunneling over 100 feet into the dark solid core, lighted only by flares, the men were discouraged to the point of despair. The flares consumed the oxygen in the narrow cavern and the men were becoming ill.

Then, as they pounded the limestone with their battering rams, they heard the muffled sound of something falling. The sound came from the east of their bore. With renewed vigor they now worked excitedly toward the direction of the sound. Soon they broke into a hollow, steep, angular passage. On the floor before them lay a large angular stone that had just been dislodged from the ceiling. Instinctively they looked up to see from whence it had fallen. There above them was what seemed to be the beginning of a smoothly hewn passageway, but it was completely filled with a tightly fitting mass of red and black granite.

In all of Al Mamoun's studies of the Great Pyramid, he had found no mention of any upward passages. He realized that he had found a secret passage, hidden since the time of the Pyramid's construction, by that huge block of granite, and sealed by the angular piece of limestone that had fallen.

The men chipped away at the block of granite in an attempt to gain access to the passageway, but to no avail. So they bored through the softer limestone that surrounded it, only to find a second granite block, plugging the passageway. They tunneled around it and found a third granite block. After tunneling around that, they finally emerged into an upward passage, so small that it required crawling on hands and knees. After maneuvering their way about 150 feet up the passage, they finally emerged into a large opening where they could stand erect.

They were, in fact, the first men to enter the upward passage system since the time of the Great Pyramid's construction.

After exploring the horizontal passage that led to what is now called the Queen's Chamber, and finding it empty, they climbed the great high-ceilinged passage that led to a large room made completely of polished red granite, known today as the King's Chamber. In one end of the room was an open red granite box. Thinking that it would contain the treasure they sought, they rushed toward it. In amazement and disappointment, they found it completely empty—no celestial maps, no gold or jewels, and no mummy.

They reasoned, from their own difficulty in circumventing the three massive granite plugs, that had sealed the lower passageway, that it must have been sealed by the builders and that no man had ever entered the upper chambers since. So why did it not contain a mummy? And if the lid had been removed, why could it not be found within the chamber, for surely it would have been too large to fit through the narrow passageways; for the small, narrow entrance passage into the chamber had again required crawling on hands and knees. Al Mamoun came to the obvious conclusion that the chamber had been built *around* the granite box and that it had never contained a mummy nor a lid.

No lid, or pieces of a lid, have ever been found. If there had been a lid, it could not have been removed, for the passageways were too small for its transport. It could not have been broken into small pieces and removed, for there would have been no way to transport the necessary tools up through the Well, which would have been the only possible means of access. This small narrow Well shaft, when Al Mamoun found it, was completely filled with construction debris, rock chunks, and bat dung. In fact, it was not made possible to climb up through the Well until the early 1800s when it was cleared by Captain G. B. Caviglia.

Even after the Well shaft had been cleared of rubble left by the builders, it was nearly impossible to ascend. To climb the dark steep and narrow shaft required the support of a rope dropped from above. Even if this shaft had been left open at the time of the completion of construction, subsequent marauders would have required support from above to climb it, and would have had the insuperable task of transporting their tools upward; thus they would have had to break up the lid of the granite box, and retrace the same route, back down through the impossibly narrow, steep Well—an engineering feat unrivaled even by the forced entrance of Al Mamoun. And, I might add, if such marauders desired to remove a mummy, they would have had to use the same procedure, which, at this point, obviously becomes a self-defeating hypothesis.

No! It never contained a mummy, and the granite box never had a lid. The Great Pyramid was not a tomb! Yet the tomb theory still prevails.

On November 4, 1992, the famed television series, Nova, aired a program entitled "This Old Pyramid." The writers of the program based their story on the assumption that the Great Pyramid was the tomb of Khufu. They theorized that the pit at the bottom of the descending passage was first built for use as the burial chamber, but because of the stresses in the rock, the builders changed their minds and decided to make the burial chamber up higher, thus they made the ascending passages. Having placed the burial box in the top chamber, and having placed the mummy of Khufu into the box, the men then slid giant granite stones down the ascending passage to block its entrance, in the effort to prevent grave robbers from entering. Then the men climbed down the Well and escaped out through the descending passage. In Nova's program, they used a diagram showing the granite stones being dropped into place in the ascending passage.

However, when Al Mamoun and his workmen discovered the ascending passage in A.D. 820, they found that the granite blocks were so tightly wedged into the passage that there was no possible way to remove them. They had been built into the original construction of the passage. To this day, no one has been able to remove them. The only way would be to break them into small pieces and remove them a piece at a time. The concept of sliding them down the passage becomes a physical impossibility. They are simply too big for the passageway.

Also, if these three huge granite boulders had indeed been slid down the ascending passage, to seal it from grave robbers, it presupposes that these three gigantic pieces of granite were stored somewhere in an upper chamber or passage, waiting for the event of the placing of the mummy in the upper chamber, before sliding them down the passage. There is no place in the passage system large enough to have stored them. And if they had been stored in the upper passage, it would have been impossible to get a mummy in past them because the huge granite stones would have blocked the passage. They could not have been stored in the top chamber (King's Chamber) because they would not fit through the narrow, low, horizontal passage that leads to the chamber.

Nova went on to solve the problem they had created by blocking the passageway—how to get the workmen out? The program showed them climbing down through the Well and escaping out through the descending passage. It may have been possible for men to have escaped in this manner, however, I do not believe their tools of construction would have been able to make the descent. Surely those tools would, of necessity, have been left in the upper passages or chambers. To descend through the Well would have required using a rope from above, one man at a time, through an opening just barely wide enough for him to maneuver both hands and both feet necessary to make a safe descent. However, when Al Mamoun found it, the Well was completely filled with construction debris, which evidenced that those who had completed the job had not escaped through the Well.

Thus, Nova's theory that it was the burial place of Khufu becomes a physical impossibility.

If the granite box in the King's Chamber was larger than the passage leading to the chamber, then how did they get it in there? The answer, of course, is obvious. The chamber was built around the box, the same as the first ascending passage was built around the granite plugs.

And how did the workmen get out with all their tools and stone masonry equipment? There was only one way they could have escaped—out through the top, which had not yet been completed. The whole structure was built from the bottom upward, thus the construction of the King's Chamber would have been completed by the placement of the roof. This would have been followed by the building of the construction chambers above the roof, which diffused the downward pressure from the weight of the stones to be placed above.

But why belabor the point that it was not a tomb?

I feel it is vital to the understanding of the symbolism of the Pyramid. In the first place, it is important to realize that the Great Pyramid has global, universal and prophetic significance, and it is degrading to the importance and majesty of the structure to bring it down to the product of the pride of an ancient Pharaoh. Secondly, by ascribing it to the aggrandizement of a mere human, we totally miss the message it preserves for all mankind—the message of a plan of salvation through Christ Jesus, and mankind's return to oneness with his Creator.

If it was not a tomb, then why the granite box in the King's Chamber that looks strangely like a sarcophagus, and is the appropriate size to have contained a mummy?

The box has the appearance of a tomb, but was found open and empty. All the evidence suggests that it was left that way by the builders—open and empty.

The prophet Isaiah spoke of the Great Pyramid as being a *"witness"* in the land of Egypt. A witness of what? A witness to whom? This mysterious, empty, lidless granite box in the King's Chamber is a witness of the greatest event in the history of humanity—the resurrection of Jesus!

This is more than a mere assumption; it is the result of an examination of the geometry of that box. It tells its own story, and needs no interpretation, nor even any assumptions.

First, let's look at the area of the entire inner surface of the box, not including a lid. Amazingly it measures .0001480 of a square furlong. I mention this square measure first because it covers the entire interior surface—the closest we can come to what would have been in the box, if it had indeed contained anything. The number 1480, as already noted, is the gematria for Christ (the Greek word for Messiah), $X\rho\iota\sigma\tau o\varsigma$.

Perhaps to get even closer to the "contents," let's take both of the cubic diagonals of the interior, measured in reeds. The measure is 1.408 reeds—the number value of *Saviour, $\sigma\omega\tau\eta\rho$,* 1408.

Or, to get the whole of its inside, let's take its cubic capacity. It is indeed .000000000281 of a cubic mile. Jesus was the real Passover Lamb, slain on the afternoon of the Passover, and his name of *Lamb, $\alpha\rho\nu\iota o\nu$,* has a number value of 281.

We can also break down the dimensions of the box to its various sides. For instance, the perimeter of one end of the interior is 122.1 inches. It is most appropriate, if this box represents his open tomb, that the Greek word *carcase, $\pi\tau\omega\mu\alpha$,* spoken of in Matthew 24:28 as representing Jesus, has a number value of 1221. The prophecy concerning his birth in Isaiah 9:6 said his name would be called *Wonderful.* This prophecy in the Septuagint (a Greek version of the Old Testament) spells the name $\Theta\alpha\upsilon\mu\alpha\sigma\tau o\varsigma$, which has a number value of 1221.

Twice this number (the perimeter of both ends of the interior), would be 244.2 inches, which is the number value for *The Son of God, $\tau\eta$ $\upsilon\iota o\upsilon$ $\tau o\upsilon$ $\Theta\varepsilon o\upsilon$,* 2442.

The side measures also bear his name. The square measure of both sides of the interior is .00000133 of a square mile. *Christ,* by another spelling, $X\rho\iota\sigma\tau o\nu$, has the number value of 1330. *Lord, $K\upsilon\rho\iota\omega$,* bears the number 1330. This, of course, was an empty box, representing the open tomb, so it is most fitting that when the three women went to his tomb on Easter morning, they found it empty; but an angel who stood in the entrance of the tomb announced to them, *"He is risen," $\eta\gamma\varepsilon\rho\theta\eta$,* and it bears the number 133.

Another evidence that this empty, lidless box respresents a resurrection is the measure of the perimeter of the end of the interior in reeds. It measures .963 of a reed; and the Greek word translated *resurrection, $\alpha\nu\alpha\sigma\tau\alpha\sigma\iota\varsigma$,* in the New Testament has a number value of 963.

This is but a small portion of the measures of that granite box that have a relationship to Jesus and his resurrection. In *The Magnificent Numbers of the Great Pyramid and Stonehenge,* thirty eight such correspondencies are shown, demonstrating beyond a reasonable doubt the symbolism intended. It appears to be a tomb, but one which does not hold death. For two thousand years it rested in silent eloquence, not the repository of death, but a silent witness of the greatest event the human race has ever known. On the 16th day of the month Nisan, in the year A.D. 33, the silent symbol became a glorious reality. The grieving women who went to the tomb in the pre-dawn darkness to anoint the body of Jesus, found only an empty tomb.

The Apostle Peter, reflecting on the importance of the event exclaimed:

> ...whom God hath raised up, having loosed the pains of death: because it was not possible that he should be holden of it. For David speaketh concerning him "...thou wilt not leave my soul in hell (hades, grave), neither wilt thou suffer thine Holy One to see corruption."
> (Acts 2:25)

Surely that empty, open, lidless granite box in the Great Pyramid stands as a silent witness that Jesus indeed fulfilled the words spoken by King David, and quoted by Peter, for the Greek words used by Peter, *ουκ εγκαταλειψεις την ψυχην μου εις αδην ουδε δωσεις τον οσιον σου ιδειν διαφθοραν,* have the number value of 8696; and there are 8,696 square megalithic yards in the entire surface area of the interior of the box. Its entire empty interior speaks to us and proclaims *"thou wilt not leave my soul in hell, neither wilt thou suffer thine Holy One to see corruption,"* (Acts 2:25).

What a remarkable box! For four thousand years it held its precious secret. Now, by its dimensions, its construction, and its placement in the King's Chamber of the Great Pyramid, that granite box tells the world that there is indeed a resurrection of the dead.

The King's Chamber, by its construction, tells us that it is a life chamber, not a death chamber; for it has air vents leading to the outside. The volume of the rectangular room is 2232 cubic royal cubits. It is the gematria for *"Jesus Christ the righteous," Ιησουν Χριστον δικαιον,* (I John 2:1). It resolves to 9, showing its wholeness and perfection, and it is 12 times the speed of light (12 x 186 = 2232).

In fact, according to Adam Rutherford[1] the volume of the entire Pyramid is 37,000,000 cubic feet. A number that has great significance, for 37 is a prime that is basic to the gematria of the names of both Jehovah and his Son, Jesus Christ, as used throughout the Old and New Testaments. Chapter 5 will be devoted to an examination of the number 37 and its beauty in relation to creation.

This gigantic structure, with a volume of 37,000,000 cubic feet, was once covered with beautiful, smooth, white casing stones, which reflected the sun's rays and earned it the name *"The Light."*[2] It was also called *"The Pyramid of Light"* by the ancients. The Oxford scholar, W. Marsham Adams, wrote: "Nobly indeed does this stupendous monument respond to its sacred title of *The Light."*

Author Francis W. Chapman, in *The Great Pyramid of Ghizeh,* wrote:

> From long distances, on almost every hand, man had only to gain a trifling eminence and he saw in the sunshine, at this centre of the Earth, the Holy Pyramid, in and out and throughout, the emblem of Deity, the acme of achievement, of light, heavenly and human,

---

1   Adam Rutherford, *Pyramidology, Book I,* Institute of Pyramidology, Hertfordshire, England, 1970, p. 27.

2   In the ancient Egyptian *Book of the Dead,* the Great Pyramid is called *The Light;* its interior passages and chambers were called *The Secret Places of the Hidden God;* the Well shaft was called *The Well of Life.*

spreading its message of aspiration, and visibly reflecting the centre and source of life. Contrasting man's social surroundings with its magnificence, I think we may conclude that the Pyramid was calculated to serve as an age-long "World Light."

This appellation, *The Light,* was also used of Jesus. John called him *"The Light."* The number 37 applies to both. First, the number 370 is the gematria for the Hebrew word שלם, which, in our English Bibles is translated by the words, *perfect, whole,* or *made perfect.* The Greek word having the same meaning also bears the same number—*whole, ολος,* 370.

In the Bible, Jesus is called the *"only begotten"* Son of God. The Greek word for *only begotten, μονογενη,* has a number equivalent of 296, which is 8 x 37. The Hebrew word for *only begotten,* יחידה, has a number value of 37. To those who study the gematria of the scriptures, a word which bears the same number in both Hebrew and Greek is of special interest, for it confirms the intended number and emphasizes its importance.

Light from the sun takes 8 minutes to reach the earth, and it is not a coincidence that the title *"only begotten,"* which bears both the numbers 296 (8 x 37) and 37, relates to the distance that light comes to the earth from the sun in the same way that a circle relates to its diameter.

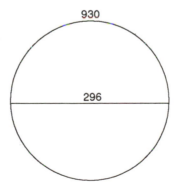

The Apostle John said, *"For God so loved the world, that he gave his only begotten Son, that whosoever believeth in him should not perish but have everlasting life,"* (3:16). This love was a special kind of love, never before known to man—it was called αγαπη, *agape,* and it bears the number 93, the same number that defines the distance light comes to us from the sun.

The number 37, that defines the cubic volume of the Great Pyramid, is the gematria for *temple, οικος*—and it surely was a grand temple. It is also the gematria for *God,* אלהא—and surely His power and greatness is reflected there. In fact, the concept of *great power,* אול has the value of 37.

The Great Pyramid was an illustration of the way to life through Jesus Christ, and the gematria for *"the way everlasting,"* דרך עולם (Psalm 139:24) is 370. The two upper chambers represent a condition of everlasting righteousness; and *"everlasting righteousness,"* צדק לעולם (Psalm 119:142) also bears the number 370.

One of the secrets of the Great Pyramid that has puzzled man from as far back as we have any records, is the missing topstone. There is no record that it was ever placed on the summit of that magnificent monument. The ancient historians who saw it before it was stripped of its beautiful white casing stones tell us that it had no topstone. There are also indications in the Bible that it was never placed. To date, no one has ever found it. Some say it was once covered with gold, which is only conjecture, but a very reasonable one, in view of its symbolism. It has been suggested that it is perhaps buried somewhere near the Great Pyramid, and that when that which the Pyramid symbolizes is accomplished, it will be found and raised to its rightful position on the summit of that glorious monument.

The topstone would have been the only stone in the entire structure that was itself a perfect pyramid, with the same proportions as the complete Pyramid. This topstone would have been enormous. Each side would have a length of 572.2 Pyramid inches, or about 48 feet, and its height would have been about 30 feet. As a single stone it would have been

70

colossial! No wonder it was never lifted into place; and it causes some to question if it ever will be. That this enormous mass of rock—the perfect topstone—should represent Jesus is referred to in both the Old and New Testaments.

Psalm 118:22 & 23 suggests that the stone was never placed by the builders, but that which it represents is indeed placed at the top by God. It reads, *"The stone which the builders refused is become the head-stone of the corner."* The Hebrew for *"the head-stone of the corner,"* לראש פנה has the number value of 666.[1]

This may startle some, that the head-stone which represents Jesus Christ would have the number that is usually associated with the anti-christ, 666. However, the anti-christ has that number by usurpation; it originally belonged to Christ. That it should be used with reference to the topstone of the structure that was once known as *"The Light,"* is fitting, for the origin of light, in Genesis 1:14, has a number value of 666— יהי מארת, *"Let there be lights."*

We saw how this topstone also represented the sun, the source of light, in relation to the Pyramid's square base. The sun, of course, represents Jehovah, the true source of light and life. Thus the prophet Isaiah (42:5) spoke of *"Jehovah God that created the heavens,"* האל יהוה בורא השמים, 666. The number resolves to 9, showing the wholeness of the Creator and that which was created.

Another reference to the topstone of the Great Pyramid is found in Zechariah 4:7—*"He shall bring forth the top-stone with shoutings, Grace! Grace be to it!"* הראשה תשאות חן חן לה הוציא את האבן, which adds to 2340. This has reference to Jesus Christ as the topstone— *"The Word of the Lord,"* בדבר יהוה, 234. And again a reference to Jehovah, *"I am Jehovah and there is none else,"* אני יהוה ואין עוד, gives the number 234. This also resolves to 9.

---

1   This reads *"head of the corner"* in Hebrew. The word *"stone"* has been supplied by the translators, which is indeed the correct thought.

Again, mention of the topstone can be found in Isaiah 28:16: *"Therefore thus saith the Lord God, behold, I lay in Zion for a foundation a stone, a tried stone, a precious corner-stone, a sure foundation."* At first this seems to be self contradictory, for how can a foundation be a topstone? Only in a pyramid can this be true. This topstone is called *"a precious cornerstone, a sure foundation,"* פנת יקרת מוסד מוסד, and it has a number value of 1460; a number full of meaning in the gematria of the Bible.

The gematria for קום is 146 and the word means to *raise up* or *to exalt.* It seems fitting, for this stone must be raised up to its lofty position as the crowning stone of the Pyramid, just as Jesus said, *"If I be lifted up I will draw all men unto me."* The number 146 also has to do with things *everlasting* and *eternal,* as is the thought in the Hebrew word עולם, 146. The number also has reference to *"My Son,"* τον υιον μου, 1460 (Mark 12:6), meaning Jesus.

This glorious topstone is represented by the number 146, and how fitting that *"the glory of the Lord shall be revealed,"* נגלה כבוד יהוה, also bears the number 146 (Isa. 40:5). David, in Psalm 27:4, spoke of the time when *"the King of glory shall come in,"* יבוא מלך הכבוד, which has a number equivalent of 146.

This number also has reference to Jehovah in his position of king, such as:

146	*The King, Jehovah,* למלך יהוה,	(Zech. 14:17)
146	*Jehovah-nissee,* יהוה נסי,	(Ex. 17:15)
146	*Our King,* מלכנו,	(Psalm 89:18)
1460	*Heavenly Father,* πατηρ ο ουρανιος,	(Matt. 6:4)
1460	*Thou, whose name alone is Jehovah, art the Most High over all the earth,* אתה שמך יהוה לבדך עליון על כל הארץ, (Psalm 83:18)	

The height of this topstone is 14.6 sacred cubits, the cubit of the Pyramid. The four angular sides have a combined measure of 14.6 reeds; and two of those angular sides measure .0146 of a mile. The relationship of the geometry to the gematria is not by chance.

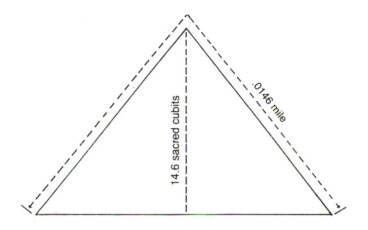

The topstone, representing the Elohim, both Father and Son, is shown in another graphic illustration, connecting it with the sun.

The sun is, in fact, an orb of fire that is used metaphorically to show the power of God. In the book of Hebrews (12:29) is the statement *"Our God is a consuming fire,"* και γαρ ο Θεος ημων πυρ καταναλισκον, which has a number value of 2720. Its connection with the topstone is obvious in the gematria of Psalm 118:22—*"The stone which the builders rejected,"* אבן מאסו הבונים, 272. This number is very close to the solar number, for the diameter of the sun, 864,000 miles, gives a circumference of 2,714,334 miles.

If 272 were used as one side of a square, the perimeter would be 1088, which is the gematria for *"He shall bring forth the headstone,"* והוציא את האבן הראשה, (Zech. 4:7). Further identification is made in Psalm 124:8 *"Jehovah who made the heaven and earth,"* יהוה עשה שמים וארץ, which adds to 1088.

In I Peter 2:6 & 7 we have been given a graphic word picture of this topstone having been rejected by the builders:

> *Behold I lay in Zion a chief cornerstone, elect and precious: and he that believeth on him shall not be confounded. Unto you therefore which believe, he is precious; but unto them which be disobedient, the stone which the builders rejected, the same is made the head of the corner.*

This *"stone which the builders rejected,"* δε λιθος ον απεδοκιμασαν οι οικοδομουντες, by the rules of gematria, bears the number 2320, the same as *"Let there be light,"* יהי אור, 232, in Genesis 1:3. He is *"The Word of the Lord,"* דבר יהוה, 232, in Isaiah 1:10; and he is *"the One who is, who was, and who is to come,"* ο ων και ο ην και ο ερχομενος, 2320, in Revelation 1:4. The identification of Jesus with the topstone of the Pyramid and with light is unmistakable.

This relationship is shown in the geometry of that topstone. Using the numbers found in the scriptural references to the topstone, the relationship to Jesus Christ and to light are convincing evidence of the intent of the Architect.

Let's draw a topstone whose height is *"chief cornerstone,"* ακρογωνιαιον, 1184 (I Pet. 2:6); the base of that topstone would be 186, relating to the speed of light. Four times the base of 186 (making a square) would be a perimeter of 744. The number value of *"Two great lights,"* המאורת הגדלים, is 744. A circle with the same circumference as the square would touch the top of this chief cornerstone, and would have a diameter of 236.8. The gematria for *Jesus Christ, Ιησους Χριστος,* is 2368. The base of this rock, being 186, is the diameter of a circle whose circumference is 584, which is the gematria for *"the God and Father of our Lord Jesus Christ,"* Θεος και πατηρ του κυριου ημων Ιησου Χριστου, (I Pet. 1:3).

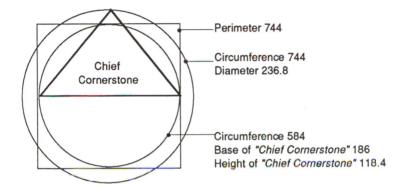

The smaller circle in the above diagram could also represent earth's mean orbit around the sun, which has a diameter of 186 million miles.

The two angular sides of this *"Chief Cornerstone"* would be 301. This is a most interesting number. It is the gematria for *"He is the Rock,"* הצור, 301 (Deut. 32:4), as well as being the gematria for *"foundation,"* אש. It is also the number value of *Calvary, κρανιον,* 301, the place where Jesus was crucified.

These are not the actual dimensions of the topstone, they are proportional, based on the gematria of *"Chief Cornerstone,"* which is 1184. The same proportional model can be made of the entire Pyramid, including its topstone. Using the reed as the measuring unit, and the Pyramid at its rock level base, the width of one side is 432 reeds. The height of the Pyramid to its apex is 275 reeds, the diameter of the large circle becomes 550 reeds, and its circumference 1728 reeds. These are actual measures. What a beautiful story these dimensions tell!

432 reeds—width of Great Pyramid at rock level
432,000 miles—radius of the sun
432   *All things* (the universe), $\pi\alpha\nu\tau\alpha$, (Rev. 21:5)
432   *World*, תבל, (Psalm 96:13)
432   *Foundation*, $\kappa\alpha\tau\alpha\beta o\lambda\eta$
432   *A great sign* (wonder), $\sigma\eta\mu\varepsilon\iota o\nu\ \mu\varepsilon\gamma\alpha$
432   *You are Jehovah*, אתה יהוה, (Isa. 37:20)
432   *The Saviour* (Jehovah), מושיעו, (Jer. 14:8)
432   *Thy house* (Jehovah's), ביתך, (Psalm 65:4)

275 reeds—height of Great Pyramid from rock level
2750 *The Lord's Christ*, $\tau o\nu\ X\rho\iota\sigma\tau o\nu\ K\nu\rho\iota o\nu$, (Luke 2:26)

550 reeds—diameter of circle reaching to apex of Pyramid
55   *Lord*, אדן
550   *Holy*, $o\sigma\iota o\varsigma$
5500 *One God and Father of all, who is above all, and through
      all, and in you all*, $\varepsilon\iota\varsigma\ \Theta\varepsilon o\varsigma\ \kappa\alpha\iota\ \pi\alpha\tau\eta\rho\ \pi\alpha\nu\tau\omega\nu\ o\ \varepsilon\pi\iota$
      $\pi\alpha\nu\tau\omega\nu\ \kappa\alpha\iota\ \delta\iota\alpha\ \pi\alpha\nu\tau\omega\nu\ \kappa\alpha\iota\ \varepsilon\nu\ \pi\alpha\sigma\iota\nu$, (Eph. 4:6)

1728 reeds—circumference of circle reaching to apex of Pyramid
1728 *True Light* (referring to Jesus), $\phi\omega\varsigma\ \alpha\lambda\eta\theta\iota\nu o\nu$, (John
      1:9)
1728 *Holy Jerusalem* (the New Jerusalem), $\alpha\gamma\iota\omega\nu$
      $I\varepsilon\rho o\nu\sigma\alpha\lambda\eta\mu$, (Rev. 21:10
1728 *Deep and secret things*, עמיקתא ומסתרתא, (Dan. 2:22)

Surely all that is contained within that circle are *"deep and
secret things,"* 1728; however the message it has for man—the
message of salvation through Christ—is one to be proclaimed,
(*proclaim*, $\kappa\eta\rho\nu\sigma\sigma\omega$, 1728).

4
Through the Window

The visitor to Stonehenge today, walking amid those towering monoliths, realizes that he is looking through windows at the distant landscape. The archways of the Sarsen Circle and the Trilithons offer him fleeting glimpses of these vistas as he walks through those 4,000-year old circles. But what does he see? Were those windows focused on anything out there?

At the time Stonehenge was built, the bank, which was six feet high, served as a horizon for anyone of normal height. This makes unnecessary the search for the distant view, for something out there. It also makes the only view a celestial one. Indeed, the visual alignments at Stonehenge were precisely focused on the risings and settings of the sun and moon. These alignments still generally work today, even though the artificial horizon is no longer high enough to function as such; and even though the apparent positions of the sun have moved slightly, due to the precession of the equinoxes. The view through the windows still functions as a solar and lunar observatory.

Regarding these *"two great lights,"* the Genesis account of creation tells us:

> *And God said, Let there be lights in the firmament of the heaven to divide the day from the night; and let them be for signs, and for seasons, and for days, and years."* (Gen. 1:14)

77

A clue to the meaning of the signs is in its gematria. *"And let them be for signs, and for seasons and for days and years,"* has a total numerical value of 1306. This is the number given to Jesus, hidden in the name *Emmanuel,* which means *"God with us,"* μεθ ημων ο Θεος, 1306.

The *sun, ηλιος,* 318, and the *moon, σεληνη,* 301, when added, become 619 (318 + 301 = 619). A circle with a circumference of 619 has a diameter of 197. The name *Emmanuel,* עמנואל, has the number equivalent of 197.

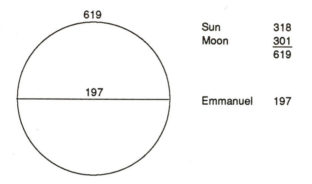

Sun	318
Moon	301
	619

Emmanuel	197

We know, and it is obvious, that the sun and moon are for the establishing of day and night, for seasons, and for years. In their relationship to earth, these appear to be their primary function. But what about *signs?* Of what are they signs?

They are signs of *"God with us,"* 1306—as was embodied in his Son, Jesus, whom God named Emmanuel. If the number 1306 were used as the circumference of a circle, the diameter would be 415.7—the number that represents Jesus in his completed work of the redemption and restoration of man: *"King of kings and Lord of lords,"* βασιλευς βασιλεων και κυριος κυριων, 4157 (Rev. 19:16). The relationship of the numbers appears to be intentional, for the whole story of the Bible, from Genesis to Revelation, is about the redemption and restoration of man.

If then, the sun and moon are for signs that point to Jesus and the work of redemption and restoration, how do we identify such signs?

At Stonehenge, as we have seen, the relationship of the Sarsen Circle to the Bluestone Circle is identical to that of the New Jerusalem; the latter being a picture of the completed work of redemption and restoration. Even the numbers are the same, but on a different scale. When a common scale is used, the one overlays the other precisely.

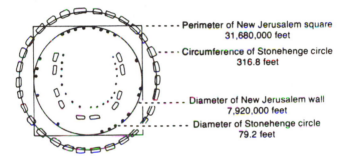

Perimeter of New Jerusalem square
31,680,000 feet

Circumference of Stonehenge circle
316.8 feet

Diameter of New Jerusalem wall
7,920,000 feet

Diameter of Stonehenge circle
79.2 feet

If we were to draw the earth and moon on the same scale, they would also overlay Stonehenge and the New Jerusalem with precision, with the added feature of the exact proportions of the Great Pyramid constructed on the diameters of earth and moon. That any two of these would, by coincidence, overlay with precision is unlikely, but that all four should overlay on such a grand scale as being earth-commensurate, is evidence of a Master Architect!

It was indeed the work of a Master Architect. The combined diameters of earth and moon are 10,080 miles, and it is the gematria for *"The work of thy fingers,"* מעשה אצבעתיך, 1008, (Psalm 8:3).

The fact that these *"signs"*—Stonehenge, the New Jerusalem, Earth, Moon, Sun, and the Great Pyramid—all bear the same numbers in their geometry, leads us not only to marvel, but to inquire further as to the message these signs are declaring.

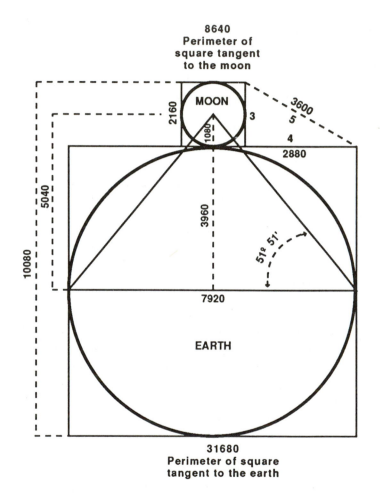

8640
Perimeter of
square tangent
to the moon

MOON

3

3600
5

4

2880

2160

1080

5040

10080

3960

7920

51° 51'

EARTH

31680
Perimeter of square
tangent to the earth

Distances are in miles.

80

The geometry of this simple diagram is astounding. The pyramid that can be constructed on the diameters of earth and moon bears the precise proportions of the Great Pyramid. The circle that represents the earth, is also commensurate by both number and proportion to the Bluestone Circle at Stonehenge and the wall of the New Jerusalem. The square drawn tangent to the earth is commensurate by both number and proportion to the Sarsen Circle at Stonehenge, and the ground plan of the New Jerusalem. Since the light of the moon is the reflected light of the sun, both are shown: the moon is shown by the circle, whose diameter is 2160, yet the square drawn tangent to that circle has for its perimeter the solar number, 8640.

The message in the *signs* can be obtained from the gematria. Let's begin with the diameter of the earth, 7,920 miles. The number is identified with *"Jehovah, the maker of the heavens,"* יהוה עשה שמים, 792 (Psalm 121:2). This was wrought through His *"great power,"* μεγαλη δυναμις, 792 (Acts 8:10). Man was placed on this earth and given dominion over it. His rulership was God-given, as the Psalmist wrote, *"You made him to rule,"* תמשילהו, 792. Having fallen through disobedience, man came under divine judgment: *"His judgments are in all the earth,"* בכל הארץ משפטיו, 792 (Psalm 105:7). A redeemer was provided, offering *"salvation,"* ישועות, 792, (Psalm 116:13); and thereby the earth can once more be a part of the *"Kingdom of God,"* βασιλειαν Θεου, 792, (Matt. 21:31).[1]

The square drawn tangent to the earth has a perimeter of 31,680 miles; or, if we made the pyramid that is inscribed within it three-dimensional, its square base would measure 31,680 miles. The pivotal character in bringing salvation to man, and the establishing of the Kingdom of God, is the *Lord Jesus Christ, Κυριος Ιησους Χριστος,* 3168. For this to be accomplished, he must become the *"Mediator between God and man,"* μεσιτης Θεου και ανθρωπων, 3168, (I Tim. 2:5).

---

1 By the rules of gematria, *colel* has been added or subtracted from some of these numbers.

The moon has a diameter of 2,160 miles. It is fitting that the topstone of this inscribed pyramid reaches the center of the moon, for that topstone, *"the stone which the builders rejected,"* λιθον ον απεδοκιμασαν οι οικοδομουντες, (Mark 12:10), has a number equivalent of 2160. It is the number of *"power,"* or *"might,"* גבורה, 216—the power of rulership in the *"kingdom of the Father,"* βασιλεια των πατρος, 2160, (Matt. 13:43).

The square drawn tangent to the moon bears the solar number, 8640. These two great lights are shown by one configuration, since the light of the moon is merely the reflected light of the sun. The topstone, being the *"cornerstone,"* γωνια, 864, reaches to the middle of these two great lights. The heavenly *Jerusalem, Ιερουσαλημ,* 864, is represented here. It is *holy, αγιων,* 864. It pictures the time when *"He shall reign,"* βασιλευσει, 864, until he has put all enemies under his feet (Rev. 3:12). Then will *"the word of the Lord from Jerusalem,"* ודבר יהוה מירושלם, 864, go out through all the earth, healing and giving life, as the rays of the sun.

The apex of that glorious topstone of the Pyramid fits precisely into the very center of the sun-moon in the illustration. It represents Jesus, *"the true light that lighteth every man that cometh into the world,"* (John 1:9). It also represents God, the source of life. The radius of the moon is 1,080 miles, and the complete topstone of the figure, rests wholly within that radius. Its position atop the Pyramid represents divine rulership. And this is the thought in the number 1080.

In Isaiah 66:1 is found the statement, *"Heaven is my throne and the earth is my footstool,"* השמים כסאי והארץ הדם רגלי, which has a number value of 1080. This position of rulership is again shown in Habakkuk 2:20: *"The Lord is in his holy temple, let all the earth keep silence before him,"* קדשו הם מפניו כל הארץ יהוה בהיכל, and it has the number equivalent of 1080. The number is repeated in Isaiah 45:18, emphasizing ownership and rulership of the earth: *"God himself that formed the earth and made it,"* הוא האלהים יצר הארץ ועשה, 1080.

God told the prophet Joel, *"I will pour out my spirit upon all flesh,"* (Joel 2:28). How fitting that the *"Holy Spirit,"* πνευμα το αγιον, bears the number 1080. The healing and lifegiving rays, emanating from the glorious topstone, is the power of God's Holy Spirit, poured out upon all the earth.

The entire height of this earth-commensurate pyramid in the diagram would be 5,040 miles. It beautifully represents *"the Kingdom of our Lord and His Christ,"* βασιλεια Κυριου ημων και Χριστου αυτου, which has a number value of 5040. That kingdom will include *"all nations,"* παντα εθνη, 504, (Rev. 12:5). This restoration of the earth and man was purchased for us by Jesus as he hung upon the cross. *"They pierced my hands and my feet,"* כארי ידי ורגלי, 504, (Psalm 22:16). This is why Isaiah prophesied *"The ransomed of the Lord shall return,"* פדויי יהוה ישבן, 504—they shall be restored to that kingdom which was originally meant for mankind, which Adam lost because of disobedience. This restoration will come through *"the fountain of living waters,"* מקור מים חיים, 504, (Jer. 2:13).

The entire dimension of the diagram, which includes all of the *signs,* the sun, moon, earth, Pyramid, New Jerusalem, and Stonehenge, becomes 10,080 miles. The intention of the design by the Master Architect is beautifully displayed in the words of the Psalmist, *"The work of thy fingers,"* מעשה אצבעתיך, 1008. This is from Psalm 8:3 where David pondered, *"When I consider thy heavens, the work of thy fingers, the moon and the stars, which thou hast ordained; what is man that thou art mindful of him?"* It has reference to all the works of God.

This completed picture is beautifully portrayed in Psalm 113:4: *"The Lord is high above all nations, and His glory above the heavens,"* רם על כל גוים יהוה על השמים כבודו, which has a number value of 1008. It is also shown in the word picture of John in Revelation 15:3, *"And they sing the song of Moses, the servant of God, and the song of the Lamb."* και αδουσιν την ωδην Μωυσεως του δουλου του Θεου και την ωδην του αρνιου, which adds to 10080. This is *"when the Lord of hosts shall reign in Mount Zion,"* כי מלך יהוה צבאות בהר ציון, (Isa. 24:23), which bears the number 1008. The prophet Isaiah went on to describe that time. He said:

> *And he will destroy in this mountain (kingdom) the face of the covering, cast over all people, and the veil that is spread over all nations. He will swallow up death in victory; and the Lord God will wipe away tears from off all faces; and the rebuke of his people shall he take away from off all the earth: for the Lord hath spoken it. And it shall be said in that day, Lo, this is our God; we have waited for him, and he will save us: this is the Lord; we have waited for him. We will be glad and rejoice in his salvation. For in this mountain (kingdom) shall the hand of the Lord rest.* (Isaiah 25:7-9)

Notice all the numbers in this diagram of the *signs*—they each resolve to 9. This beautifully describes the wholeness and perfection of that promised kingdom.

7920	7 + 9 + 2 = 18	1 + 8 = 9
31680	3 + 1 + 6 + 8 = 18	1 + 8 = 9
2160		2 + 1 + 6 = 9
8640	8 + 6 + 4 = 18	1 + 8 = 9
1080		1 + 8 = 9
5040		5 + 4 = 9
10080		1 + 8 = 9

It cannot be denied that the sun and moon are *signs*, because Genesis 1:14 says they are. The New Jerusalem is described in the book of Revelation as that glorious kingdom which envelopes the whole earth. Thus, in the light of the above evidence, I can say with certainty that Stonehenge and the Great Pyramid are also *signs*, pointing to that kingdom. And with the confirmation of such evidence, we have the assurance that gematria is not a pseudo-science, but one designed by God and incorporated into his plan for the salvation and restoration of man.[1]

The cosmos, as it relates to man, *i.e.,* the earth, sun and moon, is directly related to Stonehenge by its geometry. Upon examination, it becomes apparent that the Architect of Stonehenge knew the measures of the cosmos. This has been illustrated graphically in *The Magnificent Numbers of the Great Pyramid and Stonehenge,*[2] however, I feel the illustrations are helpful in comprehending the magnitude of these relationships, so will repeat them here.

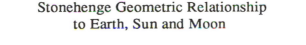

Stonehenge Geometric Relationship
to Earth, Sun and Moon

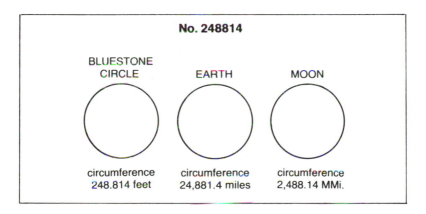

---

1 It must be acknowledged that the science of gematria is not the same as that which goes under the name of Numerology. They are two separate and distinct concepts.

2 *The Magnificent Numbers of the Great Pyramid and Stonehenge,* Bonnie Gaunt, 510 Golf Avenue, Jackson, Michigan 49203, U.S.A., $10.00.

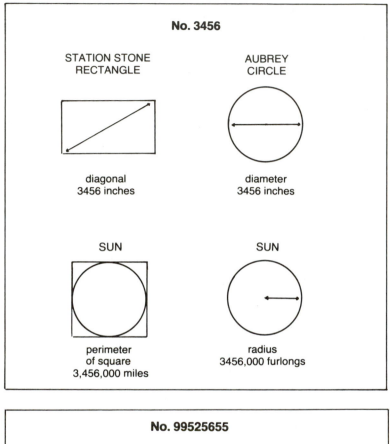

No. 3456

STATION STONE
RECTANGLE

AUBREY
CIRCLE

diagonal
3456 inches

diameter
3456 inches

SUN

SUN

perimeter
of square
3,456,000 miles

radius
3456,000 furlongs

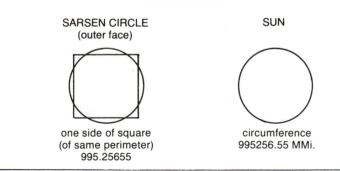

No. 99525655

SARSEN CIRCLE
(outer face)

SUN

one side of square
(of same perimeter)
995.25655

circumference
995256.55 MMi.

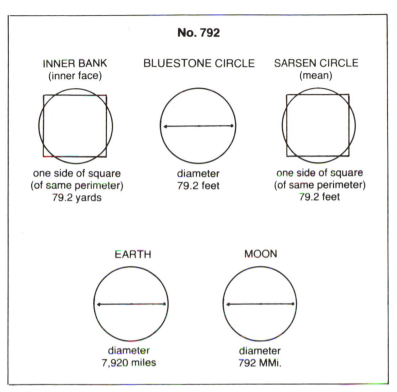

No. 792

INNER BANK
(inner face)

BLUESTONE CIRCLE

SARSEN CIRCLE
(mean)

one side of square
(of same perimeter)
79.2 yards

diameter
79.2 feet

one side of square
(of same perimeter)
79.2 feet

EARTH

MOON

diameter
7,920 miles

diameter
792 MMi.

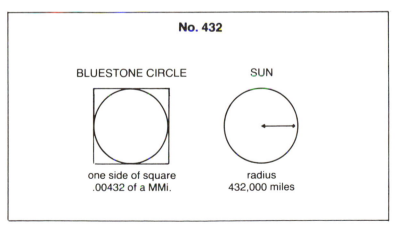

No. 432

BLUESTONE CIRCLE

SUN

one side of square
.00432 of a MMi.

radius
432,000 miles

STONEHENGE AND THE GREAT PYRAMID

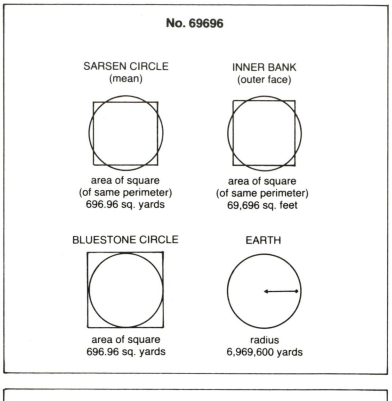

No. 69696

SARSEN CIRCLE
(mean)

INNER BANK
(outer face)

area of square
(of same perimeter)
696.96 sq. yards

area of square
(of same perimeter)
69,696 sq. feet

BLUESTONE CIRCLE

EARTH

area of square
696.96 sq. yards

radius
6,969,600 yards

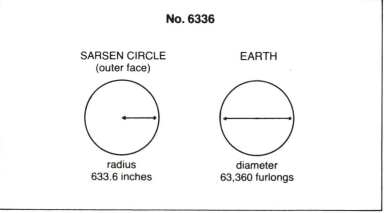

No. 6336

SARSEN CIRCLE
(outer face)

EARTH

radius
633.6 inches

diameter
63,360 furlongs

THROUGH THE WINDOW

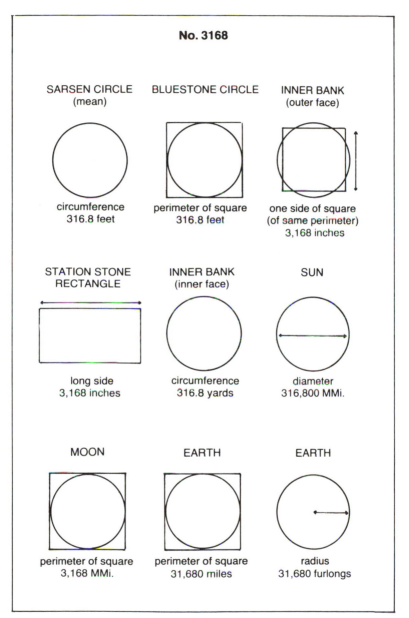

No. 3168

SARSEN CIRCLE
(mean)

circumference
316.8 feet

BLUESTONE CIRCLE

perimeter of square
316.8 feet

INNER BANK
(outer face)

one side of square
(of same perimeter)
3,168 inches

STATION STONE
RECTANGLE

long side
3,168 inches

INNER BANK
(inner face)

circumference
316.8 yards

SUN

diameter
316,800 MMi.

MOON

perimeter of square
3,168 MMi.

EARTH

perimeter of square
31,680 miles

EARTH

radius
31,680 furlongs

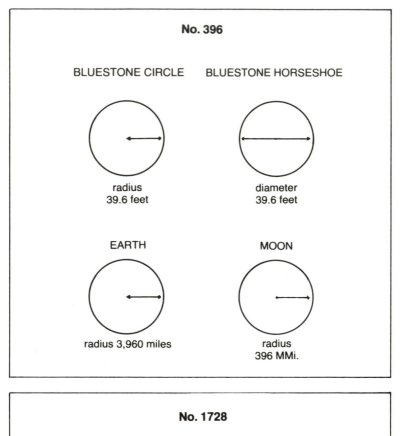

No. 396

BLUESTONE CIRCLE   BLUESTONE HORSESHOE

radius
39.6 feet

diameter
39.6 feet

EARTH   MOON

radius 3,960 miles

radius
396 MMi.

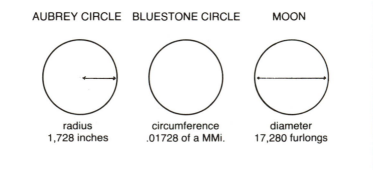

No. 1728

AUBREY CIRCLE   BLUESTONE CIRCLE   MOON

radius
1,728 inches

circumference
.01728 of a MMi.

diameter
17,280 furlongs

THROUGH THE WINDOW

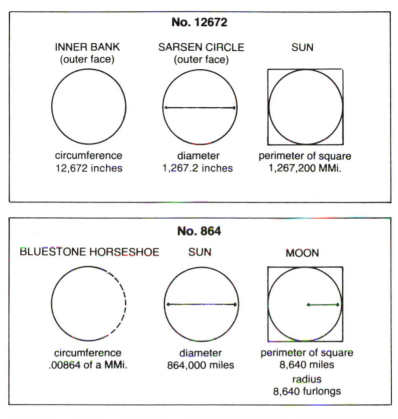

No. 12672

INNER BANK (outer face)	SARSEN CIRCLE (outer face)	SUN
circumference 12,672 inches	diameter 1,267.2 inches	perimeter of square 1,267,200 MMi.

No. 864

BLUESTONE HORSESHOE	SUN	MOON
circumference .00864 of a MMi.	diameter 864,000 miles	perimeter of square 8,640 miles radius 8,640 furlongs

No. 2160

BLUESTONE HORSESHOE	SARSEN CIRCLE (inner face)	MOON
one side of square (of same perimeter) .002160 of a MMi.	area of square .2160 of a sq. MMi.	diameter 2160 miles

No. 1452

INNER BANK
(inner face)

INNER BANK
(crest)

EARTH

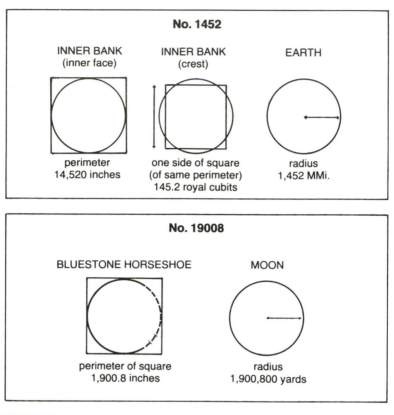

perimeter
14,520 inches

one side of square
(of same perimeter)
145.2 royal cubits

radius
1,452 MMi.

No. 19008

BLUESTONE HORSESHOE

MOON

perimeter of square
1,900.8 inches

radius
1,900,800 yards

No. 38016

SARSEN CIRCLE
(mean)

MOON

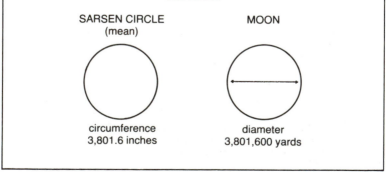

circumference
3,801.6 inches

diameter
3,801,600 yards

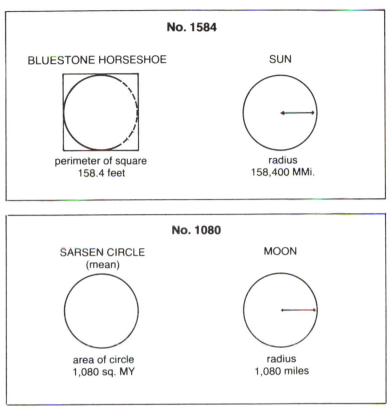

The prophet Isaiah said that the Great Pyramid would be a sign in the land of Egypt. The prophecy reads:

In that day shall there be an altar to the Lord in the midst of the land of Egypt, and a pillar at the border thereof to the Lord. And it shall be for a sign and for a witness unto the Lord of hosts in the land of Egypt. (Isaiah 19:19 & 20)

The Great Pyramid already existed in Isaiah's day, but he was pointing to a future time when it would be known that it

93

ביום	58
ההוא	17
יהיה	30
מזבח	57
ליהוה	56
בתוך	428
ארץ	291
מצרים	380
ומצבה	143
אצל	121
גבולה	46
ליהוה	56
והיה	26
לאות	437
ולעד	110
ליהוה	56
צבאות	499
בארץ	293
מצרים	380
כי	30
יצעקו	276
אל	31
יהוה	26
מפני	180
לחצים	178
וישלח	354
להם	75
מושיע	426
ורב	208
והצילם	181

Height of the Great Pyramid in
Pyramid inches, to the original
summit platform 5,449

94

was a *sign*. That Isaiah was indeed speaking of the Great
Pyramid we know by the gematria. The total number value of
that verse of scripture is 5449—the height of the Great Pyramid, from its socket base level to its summit platform is 5449
Pyramid inches.

During the many years that I have pursued the study of
gematria, I have gone through the Bible and obtained the
number equivalents of the names, phrases, concepts, etc., and
have recorded them in numerical order for reference. It was
simply the gathering of sterile information, not attempting to
"make it fit" into any pre-conceived ideas of my own. I wanted
to observe if any prominent numbers or number patterns would
emerge. It was an honest attempt to read the *signs,* with no desire
to force or create anything.

The patterns that became obvious are geometric, beginning
with simple concepts such as the circle, square and triangle, and
then becoming interwoven into an intricate and elaborate
geometrical chain. The full magnitude of the pattern is not
known to me—I only see pieces of it. But the pieces tell me that
there is a complete master pattern, of which I am only seeing
small parts. This geometric pattern is in the entire created
universe.

Evidences of geometric patterns in creation are all around
us. Common salt, for instance, always crystalizes into a cube;
the snowflake is always six-pointed; and fluoride crystals are
always little pyramids. Each shape is the result of the bonding
of its atomic structure. The resulting patterns are always consistent. Even the elaborate chain of DNA, which determines
biological form, is a consistent and predictable pattern. Geometric form and progression are basic in all created matter, and
they can all be reduced to number.

In the Bible, one of the interesting patterns that emerges
simply uses the circle and square—it is a pattern regarding the
topstone of the Pyramid and its relation to the sun and to the
divine rulership. This pattern came to my attention by the fact

that the words *"headstone," "cornerstone,"* and *"sun,"* in Hebrew all have the same number value—53; and *"Son"* in Greek
also bears the number 53.

53   *Headstone,* אבן
530   *Cornerstone,* פנת
53   *Sun,* חמה
530   *Son,* υιον

A square with sides of 53 would have a perimeter of 212.
Take this perimeter and lay it out as a straight line as the
diameter of a circle, and the circumference would be 666. I do
not believe it was coincidence that 666 is the gematria for
"Head of the corner," לראש פנה. I believe it was part of a pre-
determined pattern, because the number 666 is also the gematria
for *"Let there be lights,"* יהי מארת.

Building further on this pattern, the concept explodes into
its beauty, and the meaning of the symbol of the topstone.
Inscribe a square within the circle and it will have sides of 150.
Here we find *light, glory, power,* and *redemption!*

1500   *Light,* φως
1500   *The Lord of glory* (Jesus), (I Cor. 2:8), Κυριον της δοξης
1500   *Power,* δυναμεως
150   *Ransom,* פדיון, (also translated *redemption*)

The four sides of this square give a perimeter of 600, which
is the number pertaining to man and the earth. *World,* κοσμος,
has the number value of 600.

Graphically, the pattern looks like this (not to scale):

THROUGH THE WINDOW

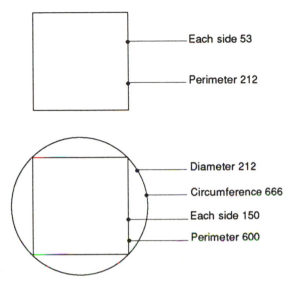

Each side 53

Perimeter 212

Diameter 212

Circumference 666

Each side 150

Perimeter 600

The pattern tells us that the topstone of the Pyramid represents light and power as was personified in the person of Jesus Christ, who gave his life as a ransom for man, that all peoples of the world might experience redemption!

But that is only part of the story. As we build, using circles and squares, more of the story is revealed, showing the relationship of the Elohim, both Father and Son, and the work of creation. The progression of the patterns shown below are not to scale, for reasons of space.

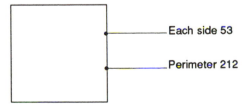

Each side 53

Perimeter 212

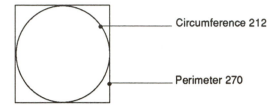

Circumference 212

Perimeter 270

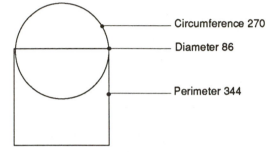

Circumference 270

Diameter 86

Perimeter 344

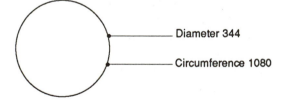

Diameter 344

Circumference 1080

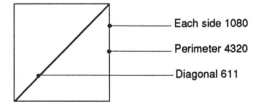

Each side 1080

Perimeter 4320

Diagonal 611

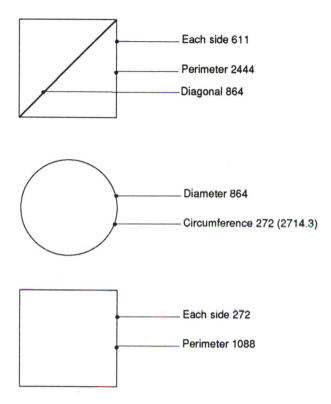

Each side 611
Perimeter 2444
Diagonal 864

Diameter 864
Circumference 272 (2714.3)

Each side 272
Perimeter 1088

To see the above pattern as it really appears, it would be one interwoven geometric figure, becoming progressively too large to fit on these pages; but the numbers tell the story.

53 *Headstone,* אבן
530 *Cornerstone,* פנת
53 *Sun,* חמה
530 *Son, υιον*

86   *Elohim,* אלהים

860   *Who hath laid its cornerstone,* או מי ירה אבן פנתה, (Job
      38:6)

86   *The majesty of Jehovah,* גאון יהוה, (Isa. 24:14)

860   *Perfection,* תכלית, (Job 11:7)

344   *Great Wonder,* μεγαλα σημεια

3440 *The Light of the world,* (Jesus), το φως του κοσμου
      (Matt. 5:14)

1080 *Heaven is my throne and the earth is my footstool,* רגלי
      השמים כסאי והארץ הדם, (Isa. 66:1)

1080 *God himself that formed the earth and made it,* הארץ ועשה
      הוא האלהים יצר, (Isa. 45:18)

1080 *The Holy Spirit,* πνευμα το αγιον

611   *A tried stone, a precious cornerstone,* בחן אבן יקר פנה אבן,
      (Isa. 28:16)

611   *Foundation,* אשיש

432   *A great sign* (wonder), σημειον μεγα

432   *All things* (universe), παντα

432   *Foundation,* καταβολη

432   *The Saviour,* מושיעו

432,000 miles—radius of the sun

2444 *The Lord your God,* Κυριος ο Θεος υμων

2444 *The beginning of creation,* αρχης κτισεως

864   *Cornerstone,* γωνια

864   *God,* Θεων

864   *God of peace,* Θεου ειρηνης

864   *God is fire,* Θεος πυρ, (Heb. 12:29)

864   *Life,* ζωην

864   *The word of the Lord from Jerusalem,* ודבר יהוה מירושלם,
      (Micah 4:2)

THROUGH THE WINDOW

864,000 miles—diameter of the sun

272 *The stone which the builders rejected* (Jesus as the
     topstone), אבן מאסו הבונים, (Psalm 118:22)
2720 *Our God is a consuming fire, και γαρ ο Θεος ημων πυρ
     καταναλισκον,* (Heb. 12:29)

1088 *He shall bring forth the headstone,* והוציא את האבן הראשה,
     (Zech 4:7)
1088 *Jehovah who made heaven and earth,* עשה שמים וארץ
     יהוה, (Psalm 124:8)
1088 *Perfect,* πληροω

    The number 27, which appears in the geometric patterns is not included in the above list. It is a very special number, having to do with the sun, with light, and with the beginning of creation, which will be discussed in chapter 5.

    The numbers tell the story; and it is a beautiful story. They tell of the beginning of creation, and of the Elohim, both Father and Son. They tell how the Son came to earth to be a ransom for man; how he was rejected the same as the topstone of the Pyramid had been rejected, and became a stone of stumbling to Israel, but would someday be raised up to his rightful position. The numbers tell the glorious promise that the holy spirit of God will be poured out upon all mankind, bringing life, and peace—and that the word of the Lord will go forth from the New Jerusalem to all mankind. The healing rays from the sun-topstone-God-Christ, will flow to all the earth.

    I stand in awe of the correlation of the numbers. It is nothing that I contrived, to make fit, nor do I have such ability. The numbers are there in God's written word, and in his creation. Indeed they are an integral part of that word and creation!

    Further evidence for the meaning of the topstone of the Great Pyramid—the *sign* and *wonder* in the land of Egypt, can be found in the gematria of the scriptures. The word *sign* or *wonder* is translated from the Greek word σημεια, which has a number value of 264. In the gospel of John (1:7) Jesus is called *"The Light,"* του φωτος, which adds to 2640—the same name as the ancients used for the Great Pyramid. If this were the length of one side of a square, the perimeter would be 1056, which is the number value for *"I form the light, I create darkness,"* ובורא חשך יוצר אור, (Isa. 45:7). The number 1056 is also the number value for *"He shall send them a Saviour, and a great one,"* מושיע ורב ישלח להם, (Isa. 19:20). The same number is used for *"The joy of thy salvation,"* ששון ישער, (Psa. 51:12). The diagonal of that square would be 373, which is the gematria for *"The Word,"* λογος, that was with God from the beginning (John 1:1).

The gematria for the topstone again forms a square by the use of the statement in Isaiah 28:16 *"a precious cornerstone, a sure foundation,"* פנת יקרת מוסד מוסד, which has the number equivalent of 1460. The number 146 is used over and over again in the gematria of the scriptures, all pertaining to the glory of the Father and the Son. One such statement is in Isaiah 40:5, *"The glory of the Lord shall be revealed,"* נגלה כבוד יהוה, 146. The loving name by which the Christian addresses God— *"Heavenly Father,"* πατηρ ο ουρανιος—bears the number 1460. If this were one side of a square, the perimeter would be 5840, which is the gematria for *"The God and Father of our Lord Jesus Christ,"* Θεος και πατηρ του Κυριου ημων Ιησου Χριστου, 5840, (I Pet. 1:3).

Let's try another square that bears some very familiar numbers. In Isaiah 8:14 are words spoken prophetically of Jesus, which uses the metaphor of the topstone of the Pyramid. Isaiah called him *"a stone of stumbling,"* ולאבן נגף, 222. The prophet Malachi (4:2) called him the Sun of Righteousness— *"unto you that fear my name shall the Sun of Righteousness arise with healing in his wings,"* יראי שמי שמש צדקה ומרפא בכנפיה חרחה לכם, and it has a number equivalent of 2220. Further identification can be found in the words of Jesus, *"I am the Alpha and Omega,"* εγω αλφα και ωμεγα, 2220. If 222 were one side of a square, the perimeter would be 888, which is the gematria for *Jesus, Ιησους;* and the diagonal of the square would be the *Almighty,* שדי, 314.

In the New Testament the Apostle Paul quoted Isaiah, calling Jesus *"a stone of stumbling,"* λιθον προσκομματος, (Rom. 9:3), and it bears the number 1360. Just as the above square bore the number of the *"Alpha and Omega,"* so this one reveals the same concept. *"I am Jehovah, the first and the last,"* אני יהוה ראשון ואת אחרנים, (Isa. 41:4), has the number equivalent of 1360. In Psalm 118:16 Jesus is called *"The Right Hand of Jehovah,"* ימין יהוה, and it also bears the number 136. If this were taken as the perimeter of a square, one side would be 340, which is the gematria for three names by which Jesus is known in the scriptures—*Shiloh,* השלה, *Lion,* ליש, and *The Branch,* נצר.

Let's draw another square, this time the measure of one side will be 124. Isaiah referred to Jesus prophetically as *"a precious cornerstone,"* פנת יקרת, (Isa. 28:16), and it has the number value of 1240. If one side of the square measures 124, the perimeter would be 496, which beautifully portrays God in *"His Majesty covers the heavens,"* כסה שמים הודו, 496, (Hab. 3:3). The diagonal would be 175, which is the number value for *"Lord of lords,"* אדני האדנים.

In Zechariah 4:7 the *"topstone,"* אבן הראשה, has a number value of 564; the same number as *"the right hand of God,"* δεξια Θεου, in I Peter 3:22, the place of authority given to Jesus. If 564 were one side of a square, the perimeter would be 2256, which is the gematria for *"spirit of Christ,"* πνευμα Χριστου, in Romans 8:9.

It could be judged, from these multiple evidences, that the geometry and gematria of the topstone clearly points to its symbolism—Father-Son-sun. This relationship is emphasized by combining the square with a circle as in the illustration below.

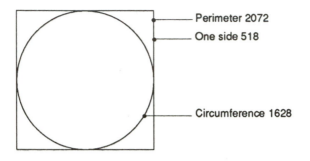

Perimeter 2072
One side 518
Circumference 1628

5180   *The stone which the builders rejected, the same is become the head of the corner,* λιθον ον απεδοκιμασαν οι οικοδομουντες ουτος εγενηθη εις κεφαλην γωνιας, (I John 4:14)

5180   *The Father sent the Son to be the Saviour of the world,* ο πατηρ απεσταλκεν τον υιον σωτηρα του κοσμου, (I John 4:14)

518   *Sun,* ηλιου

2072   *The Alpha, the Omega,* το αλφα, το ω, (Rev. 1:8)

1628   *Head of the corner,* κεφαλη γωνιας, (Matt. 21:42)
1628   *Son of David,* (Jesus), υιω Δαυιδ, (Matt. 21:15)

What a glorious topstone! Some have suggested it was covered with gold. It would have been a massive piece of rock, about 30 feet high and about 48 feet wide at its base. Although all evidence points to the theory that this topstone was never placed upon the summit of the Great Pyramid, Adam Rutherford visualized how it would have appeared, had it been placed.[1]

---

1 Adam Rutherford, *Pyramidology Book II,* Institute of Pyramidology, London, 1962, p. 259.

...what a Top-Stone! Think of its gigantic size, its tremendous weight and the fabulous cost of the gold to cover such a colossal Crowning Stone! Picture, in the brilliant sunshine, this great Top-Stone, arrayed in gold, in itself a perfect Pyramid of dazzling brilliance, towering high on the lofty summit of the massive Pyramid of snowy white—supreme magnificence indeed...!

Looking back at the sun-moon-earth model on page 80 it was illustrated that the topstone of the earth-commensurate pyramid reached the very center of the sun-moon square and circle. These *"two great lights,"* were for *signs*. The diameter of the circle representing the moon is 2,160 miles, and the square superscribed on the circle has a perimeter of 8,640, the solar number. The one configuration of circle and square appropriately illustrates that it is one light source, since the moon merely reflects the light of the sun. This light source is

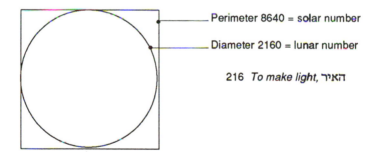

Perimeter 8640 = solar number

Diameter 2160 = lunar number

216 *To make light,* האיר

connected with another sign, of which all are familiar—the signs of the Zodiac. These signs have come down to us from ancient times. It has been suggested by Joseph A. Seiss[1] that the names and meanings of the zodiacal signs were given to Adam,

---

1 Joseph A. Seiss, *Gospel in the Stars,* Kregel Publications, Grand Rapids, MI 1972, p. 151.

Seth and Enoch, by the Creator.

These signs are basically 12, with three more for each, totaling 48. The sun, in its annual course from west to east through these constellations, passes through the 12, called the path of the ecliptic, and during that time, the moon makes 12 complete revolutions around the earth. However, the sun, at a given point of time in the year, will gradually slip back along the ecliptic path, and in 2,160 years will pass into the zone of the preceding zodiacal sign. This is called the precession of the equinoxes. This phenomenon is due to the tilt of earth's axis and the slow wobble of its rotation. Thus the sun remains in each sign of the Zodiac for 2,160 years; and the complete circuit would take 25,920 years (12 x 2160 = 25,920).

If the Sarsen Circle at Stonehenge were used to illustrate the path of the sun, its 30 upright stones would divide the circle into arcs of 12° each—representing the 12 signs. The complete circuit of 25,920 years divided by the 30 stones would give 864 years represented by each stone; 864 being the solar number. In light of all the evidence thus far presented, I cannot believe this relationship is a coincidence. The Architect of Stonehenge had a knowledge of the circuit of the heavens.

The number 27 appeared in the geometric pattern shown on page 98, which included the solar number. It proves to be a vital number relating to the sun and to creation, as will be shown in chapter 5. However, it is appropriate here to note its relationship to the path of the sun through the Zodiac.

The number 27 is a common denominator of the two great lights.

$$864 \div 27 = 32$$
$$216 \div 27 = 8$$

The total years of the path of the sun through the Zodiac is 25,920. Divide this by 27 and the result is 960. The number 96 in the gematria of the scriptures tells of the *"gift"* of God (John 4:10) by providing his Son to redeem man (*gift, δωρεαν,* 960);

it also tells the means by which that redemption was purchased—the death on the *"tree,"* $\xi \upsilon \lambda o \upsilon$, 960, (Acts 5:30). The number also tells of *"a kingdom,"* מלכו, 96, to be established on the earth (Daniel 7:14), as well as the King himself—*"I am a great King, says the Lord of hosts,"* מלך גדול אני אמר יהוה צבאות, 960.[1]

The gematria of the Elohim (Father and Son) is intricately interwoven with the two great lights, sun and moon, and the symbolism of Stonehenge and the Great Pyramid—the work of a Master Architect.

Genesis 1:14 told us that the two great lights were to divide day from night, and also be for signs, for seasons, and for days and years. It is, in fact, talking about the relationship of light to the earth.

For purposes of mapping the earth, men have covered our globe with an imaginary grid. East-west lines are called latitude, or parallels, because they are parallel to each other, and become shorter at the poles. North-south lines are called longitude, or meridians. They are all equal in length, but are farthest apart at the equator and converge at the poles.

Parallels never meet, so the distance between two lines of latitude does not change. One degree of latitude is about 69 miles. Because meridians do meet, one degree of longitude is shorter near the poles than at the equator. However, 15 degrees of longitude always equals the amount of earth that passes the sun in one hour, thus each time zone is 15°. Measuring on the mean of earth's diameter, this would be 528 miles in one hour. The 15° of longitude, of course, receives its sunlight on its

---

1 It has been suggested by Neil Pinter, Priest River, Idaho, U.S.A., that the number 960, when added to the name Lord Jesus Christ, 3168, would result in 4128—a number which chronologically spans the period from the first Adam to the second Adam; and the solar, lunar and earth numbers, 864, 216, and 792 would total 1872 years. Chronologically this would tell us that 6,000 years had elapsed between the first Adam and the date 1871 (960 + 3168 + 864 + 216 + 792 = 6000). I had not attempted to relate the gematria to chronology; however, the figures do fit the generally accepted chronology of man.

surface, the circumference, which would be 1,660 miles along the equator, considering the fact that the earth bulges at the equator and is flattened at the poles, making the equatorial circumference 24,900 miles.

These two distances, 528 and 1660 are of great significance in the relationship of earth to sun.

We have seen how the *"two great lights,"* the sun and moon, are represented by the topstone of the Great Pyramid. Referring to that glorious topstone we have the Biblical statement, *"I lay in Zion a stone,"* τιθημι εν Σιων λιθον, (I Peter 2:6), which has a number equivalent of 1660—the same as the number of miles of earth that is bathed in sunlight in one hour. Symbolically, that topstone will be raised to the lofty summit of the Pyramid when *"Jehovah shall be King,"* היהיהוה למלך, 166, (Zech. 14:9). That will be when *"the face of Jehovah,"* פני יהוה, 166, will be turned toward all mankind (Deut. 31:11). His name, *"the Most High,"* עליון, 166 will then be known by all men—a time when mankind will recognize and say *"Behold your God,"* הנה אלהיכם, 166, (Isa. 40:9), for they will walk in the sunlight, the light of his countenance.

The path of sunlight, circling the earth, if computed on the earth-diameter, would be 528 miles in one hour. This number is of the utmost significance, because it relates to the unit of measure which has come to be known as the British Statute Mile—5,280 feet. In reality, the unit was in existence long before there was a nation called Britain. Evidence of its use can be found in the measures of Noah's Ark (which will be shown in chapter 6). However, its origin is based in time and light, shown by the relationship of the sun to the speed of earth's rotation, as measured on the earth-diameter. Its relationship to sound, and therefore to time, is found in the number of vibrations per second in C above middle C in the music scale, which is 528. Its use in gematria is beautifully shown in the concept of *kingship,* or *royalty, βασιλειος,* 528.

The number 528 is exactly half the measure of the reed that was given to Ezekiel, and it is also half of each of the lintels which topped the Sarsen Circle at Stonehenge. That beautiful ring of lintels, whose mean circumference was 316.8 feet (*Lord Jesus Christ,* 3168) had an outside circumference of 331.75, making the radius of its outer face 52.8 feet. Indeed the unit we now call the British Statute Mile is from antiquity.

Artist's conception of Stonehenge at the time of its completion. This illustration shows more stones in the Bluestone Circle than probably actually existed.

Photo by Todd Alexander

Nearly all of the Great Pyramid's beautiful white casing stones have been stripped from its sides to build the capitol city of El Kaherah. In 1836, Colonel Howard-Vyse discovered a few of these casing stones under tons of rock and rubble at the base of the north face. Their enormity is shown by the size relationship to the man standing beside them.

5
In the Beginning
Elohim

The book of Genesis begins with the statement, *"In the beginning God created the heaven and the earth,"* The Hebrew word translated *"God"* in this text is *Elohim,* a plural word, implying a deity of more than one.

Throughout the first two chapters of Genesis, the creation chapters, this plural form is used. This thought of plurality is carried to the pronouns used when considering the creation of man.

And Elohim said, Let us make man in our image, after our likeness. (Genesis 1:26)

However, when obviously referring to a time when God was alone, the singular form of the word was used. *"From everlasting to everlasting thou art God,"* (Psalm 90:2). The Hebrew word is *El*—a singular word, implying that there was a time before *El* was *Elohim*. God, *El,* bears the number equivalent of 31—a prime, divisible only by 1.[1]

To the ancients, the meaning of one was unity. But something unique happens when the proportional division of unity is expressed in two terms. In geometry, this occurs only when the smaller term is to the larger term in the same way as the

---

1 Other forms of the singular deity are Elah and Eloah, both spelled אלה in Hebrew and bearing the number 36; a number that resolves to 9, representing the wholeness of the one God, before the creation of the only begotten Son.

larger term is to the smaller plus the larger. Historically this unique geometric proportion has been given the name "Golden Proportion," and in math is designated by the Greek letter ϕ (pronounced phi). To a mathematician, the Golden Proportion is written a:b::b:(a+b), thus the largest term (a+b) is a wholeness or unit composed of the sum of the other two terms. That which is divided becomes part of the whole—becomes part of unity. The ratio is 1:1.618.

Perhaps it can be more easily understood by dividing a line so that the whole line is longer than the longest section in the same proportion that the longest section is to the shorter section. Thus the wholeness of unity, though being divided into two, is nevertheless still unity. It can be simply shown by dividing a line

A   B
•————————————————————————————————•

at a point C

A   C   B
•————————————————————————•———————•

in such a way that the whole line AB is longer than
AC in the same proportion as AC is longer than CB.

This simple proportion has profoundly affected art and architecture for thousands of years. Plato called it the most binding of all mathematical relations, and the key to the physics of the cosmos. It is the relationship of the El to the Elohim. It is the division of El whereby El retains his essential wholeness and oneness. If we assigned AB the value of El, 31, it would give to CB the value of 11.84, which is the gematria for *"in a different form,"* εν ετερα μορφη.

The Greek letter ϕ, the symbol of the Golden Proportion, bears the number 500.

Just as we saw that the topstone of the earth-commensurate pyramid bore both the solar and lunar numbers, thus representing the light from the sun, so ϕ, the number 500, declares its relationship to the *"sun and moon,"* ηλιον και σεληνη, 500, in Revelation 12:1.

Phi, being a circle with a line through it, implies the division of unity. In the words of Robert Lawlor:[1]

> It is the only possible creative duality within Unity. It is the most intimate relationship, one might say, that proportional existence—the universe—can have with Unity, the primal or first division of One. For this reason the ancients called it "golden," the perfect division, and the Christians have related this proportional symbol to the Son of God.

The unity and oneness of the El and the Elohim were described by the Apostle John when telling of creation. Looking closely at the way he phrased it, we can see the geometric implications of the Golden Proportion—the division of one so that the one retains its wholeness with that which was divided. The Greek text reads, *"In the beginning was the Word, and the Word was with the God, and God was the Word."* (John 1:1)

Some add the indefinite article before *"God"* in the last phrase, rendering it *"and a God was the Word."* Since no indefinite article exists in Greek, it is added when translating into English. Whether we add the indefinite article or not, the meaning is the same. It describes the Golden Proportion.

The phrase *"the Word was with the God,"* has a deeper meaning in Greek. The word προς, here translated *"with"* is a preposition that is translated in other places as *"in"* or *"within."* For instance, in Acts 28:30, it reads *"Paul dwelt two whole years in his own hired house, and received all that came in unto (προς) him."* Again it is translated *"into"* in Acts 16:40: *"And they went out of the prison, and entered into (προς) the house*

---

1 Robert Lawlor, *Sacred Geometry,* The Crossroads Publishing Co., New York, 1982, p. 46.

of Lydia."

Realizing this meaning of the word πρoς, it is easily seen that John was alluding to the principle of the Golden Proportion when he said *"In the beginning was the Word, and the Word was with(in) the God, and (a) God was the Word."* The division of 1 retained its oneness. The Elohim—the source of all creation—was both God and the Word.

The Apostle John, using this symbol, continued: *"The same was in the beginning with the God. All things were made by him; and without him was not anything made that was made. In him was life; and the life was the light of men."* Then in verse 10 he wrote, *"He was in the world, and the world was made by him, and the world knew him not."*

Further in the same context John wrote, *"No man hath seen God at any time; the only begotten Son (Θεoς, God), which is in the bosom of the Father, he hath declared him,"* (from Marshall Diaglott). The use of Θεoς in the Greek text clearly calls him a God, within the bosom of the Father. But this God was a begotten God—begotten by the division of Unity, which retained its oneness, the Golden Proportion. This wholeness is found in the gematria of the first words of the Bible, "In the beginning Elohim," בראשׁיתאלהׁים, which has the value of 999—the ultimate concept of wholeness.

This divine proportion was incorporated into the design of both Stonehenge and the Great Pyramid. This beautiful expression of harmony and perfect proportion is shown by the height of the stones of the Sarsen Circle in relation to the circumference. The circle consists of 30 upright stones: thus if we divide the circumference by 30 we obtain the width of one upright plus the interval between. This is 10.56 feet. If we divide the height of the stones (including the lintels) by 10.56, the resulting ratio is very close to ϕ.

This beautiful proportion is also found in the Great Central trilithon. By dividing its height by its width, the result is very close to ϕ. To obtain this proportion, the builders had to sacrifice some of the stability of the stones. This is why one of the uprights of the Trilithon has fallen.

The most notable demonstration of ϕ at Stonehenge is in the relationship of the Sarsen Circle to the Bluestone Circle. The ratio between the squares of their radii is ϕ. Thus this proportion would also exist between the circumference of the earth and a square drawn on that circumference.

The Golden Proportion was built into the Great Pyramid by the relation of its angular sides to its base. It is found in the triangle formed by the height, half the base, and the apothem, which is the basic cross section of the structure.

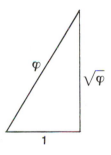

The Golden Proportion, as we have seen, is the division of 1, which retains the concept of 1—its Unity. That the Elohim (Father and Son) is represented by the number 1 is evident from the scriptures. A few examples are as follows:

100	*A great God is Jehovah,* אל גדול יהוה,	(Psalm 95:3)
1000	*Lord, Κυριου*	
1000	*Everlasting power, αιδιος δυναμις,*	(Rev 1:20)
100	*The Most High,* על	
111	*The Most High,* עליא	
111	*Wonderful,* אלף,	(Name given to Jesus in Isa. 9:6)
1111	*Name of the Son, ονομα υιου*	
1110	*Only Son, υιος μονος,*	(John 3:16)
1110	*The blood of Jesus, το αιμα Ιησου,*	(I John 1:7)

1100   *Unexcelling greatness,* υπερβαλλον μεγεθος, *(Eph.*
       1:19)

1011   *Lord of the earth,* Κυριου γη

1101   *To be equal with God,* ειναι ισα Θεω, *(Phil. 2:6)*

1101   *Creator of the ends of the earth,* בורא קצות הארץ, *(Isa.*
       40:28)

1011   *Your Redeemer, the Holy One of Israel,* וגאלך קדושישראל,
       (Isa. 41:14)

111   *The Lord of all,* אדון כל, *(Zech. 6:5)*

And I must add one more that connects this number with the sun and moon:

1001   *Two lights,* שני מארת, (sun and moon, Genesis 1:16)

The great prophecy fortelling the birth of Jesus, in Isaiah 9, exclaims *"The people who walk in darkness have seen a great light."* That *"great light"* was the one whom John called *"The true light that lighteth every man that cometh into the world."* The relationship of *"great light"* to the Elohim is shown by its gematria:

250   *Great Light,* אור גדול

250

Perimeter 1000

The Elohim declared *"I am the first, I am the last, and beside me there is no Elohim,"* (Isaiah 44:6).

Many peoples in ancient times thought the sun was God.

IN THE BEGINNING ELOHIM

Sun worship has been practiced by man throughout all the earth. And there is good reason for this. It has been obvious to man that the sun is the source of life, light and warmth. It is the biggest and brightest thing up there. Its brilliance is such that a man cannot look upon it, except as through the more dense atmospheric effect close to the horizon. It is indeed a fitting symbol of the true God.

The seemingly solid sun is actually a ball of gaseous plasma composed chiefly of hydrogen.

The atomic number for hydrogen is 1—having only one proton in its nucleus, which is orbited by one electron. This identifies it as representing the Elohim, whose number is 1. Hydrogen molecules consist of two atoms clinging together. The fusion of these two atoms releases vast amounts of energy, light and heat. Hydrogen is therefore necessary to all life on earth.

Unity creates by dividing itself. Two is not the result of putting together two ones; for one, by definition, is singular; it is Unity, therefore all inclusive. There cannot be two Ones. Unity, as the symbol of the Elohim, divides itself from within, creating a multiplicity. This is shown in the formula for relativity.

Albert Einstein drew the universe together in a simple formula: $E=mc^2$, or, mass equals energy divided by the speed of light squared—the formula for creation.

If then, all matter is energy divided by the speed of light squared, where does the energy and light come from—where is its origin? Where did God get his raw materials? Certainly, before creation began, there was nothing "out there." His raw materials came from within. It was his power and his light that was put together in the right proportion to create matter. Creation came from within the Creator. It was not the adding of ones to make many—it was the dividing of Unity.

Unity is shown by the hydrogen atom with its characteristic number 1. According to the United States Bureau of Standards, the physical constant of the hydrogen atom is 37 ÷ 27 x 100.

$$37 \div 27 = 1.370370370370 \text{ to infinity.}$$

This is an interesting equation indeed! The 1 represents the Elohim, as does also the 37, while 27 represents the sun and its resultant light; and 37 + 27 resolves back to 1.

The *"two great lights"* are multiples of 27. Thus the solar number, 864, when divided by 27 produces 32, and the lunar number, 216, when divided by 27 produces 8.

$$864 \div 27 = 32$$
$$216 \div 27 = \ \ 8$$

The Aubrey Circle of 56 holes at Stonehenge, which has been shown to be a prophetic time line, has a diameter of 288 feet. When this figure is converted to reeds it produces $288 \div 10.56 = 27.2727272727$ to infinity. Time is based in the speed of light from the sun.

If we were to multiply 37 x 27 the result is 999, the ultimate concept of wholeness in the Elohim—*"In the beginning Elohim,"* בראשית אלהים, 999. A circle with a circumference of 999 has a diameter of 318, the gematria for *sun, ηλιος.*

This relationship was shown at Stonehenge by the diameter of the Bank, which was 318 feet, forming a horizon for viewing the sun. Its circumference was 999 feet.

It is certainly not coincidence that these two numbers, 37 and 27, tell us about the Elohim, and his symbol, the sun.

$$37 \div 27 = 1.370370370370$$
$$37 \times 27 = 999$$

The sun is mostly hydrogen. The number that represents the physical constant of the hydrogen atom, when multiplied by the solar number, produces 1184, which is the gematria for *"in a different form," εν ετερα μορφη.* The reflected light of the sun, from the moon, would be represented by adding the lunar number, 216—thus the following:

118

864 x 1.370370370 = 1184
+216 x 1.370370370 = 296
1080   1480

1080 = *God himself that formed the earth and made it,*
הוא האלהים יצר הארץ ועשה
1480 = *Christ, Χριστος*

When 1080 is divided by 12, earth's foundation number, the result is 90, representing wholeness and perfection. The word *perfection* in Hebrew is כליל, and has the number value of 90.

These two numbers, 37 and 27, appear to relate to the Elohim, to light, and to the beginning of things. *Light,* אור, has the number equivalent of 207, which, by the rules of gematria is the same as 27, because zeros are merely place holders.

The physical constant of the hydrogen atom is 37 ÷ 27 x 100. As shown, the light from the moon is the reflected light from the sun, thus the lunar number, 216, is also the number of solar light. This light, when divided by the earth number, 792, produces 27, thus: 2160 ÷ 7920 = .272727272727 to infinity.

The relationship of 37 to 27 can also be shown thus:

1 ÷ 37 = .027027027027 to infinity
1 ÷ 27 = .037037037037 to infinity

These two numbers, 37 and 27, which appear to be basic to the Elohim and to light, also appear to be basic to the components of creation. As has been shown, Albert Einstein's formula, $E=mc^2$ can be converted to $m=E÷c^2$, meaning that mass (or matter) equals energy divided by the speed of light squared. The energy must come from the power of the Elohim—there is no other source; thus energy in the formula could be represented by the number 37. The speed of light is represented by the number 186. To square the speed of light we multiply 186 x 186 = 34596. Resolve the number: 3 + 4 + 5 + 9 + 6 =27. Thus the number 27 represents the speed of light squared. The formula looks like this:

$$m = E \div c^2$$
$$E = 37$$
$$c^2 = 27$$
$$m = 37 \div 27$$
$$m = 1.370370370370 \text{ to infinity}$$

Mass (matter) in Einstein's formula is the same number as the physical constant of the hydrogen atom. The formula becomes the basic process of creation—its very source and substance.

Where did God get his raw materials? His raw materials were energy and light, and they both came from within.

The first verse of Genesis reads *"In the beginning God (Elohim) created the heaven and the earth."* The Hebrew letters add to 2701. This is a remarkable figure. Why is the 1 added? The number 1, as we have seen, represents the Elohim. If this figure were divided by the common denominator 27, the result would be 100.037037037037 to infinity.

The first four words, *"In the beginning Elohim,"* has a number value of 999, which is the ultimate concept of wholeness. If we divided 2701 by 999, the result would be 2.7037037037 to infinity, giving the two basic components of creation—energy, 37, and light, 27.

These two numbers show another relationship to the sun by their multiplication:

$$2 \times 7 = 14$$
$$3 \times 7 = 21 \qquad 14 \times 21 = 294$$

294 = *The greater light* (sun), (Genesis 1:16)
המאור הגדל
(294 x 27 = 7938 resolves back to 27)

120

IN THE BEGINNING ELOHIM

The great precession of the equinoxes which marks the sun's apparent path through the Zodiac is 25,920 years. If this were divided by 960, (the Greek word *number, αριθμω,* 960) the result would be 27.

The lowest (first) number that is a multiple of both 27 and 37 is 999 (*In the beginning Elohim,* 999). If 999 were divided by 1.370370370, the result would be 729, which is the number of days and nights in one year— 365 + 364 = 729). It is an anagram of the earth number, 792.

The earthly ministry of Jesus was 1,260 days. When this is added to the period from conception to his birth, 279 days, the result is the total number of days that the *"Light of the world"* was on the earth in human form—1,539 days. Multiplied by 24, this gives 36,936 hours—a figure that resolves first to 27, and then to 9.

At this point I feel compelled to show the overwhelming evidence that the number 37 represents the Elohim, both Father and Son. I have shown the relationship to 1, now I shall show the gematria from the Old and New Testaments for the number 37. If the following list seems lengthy and burdensome, it is by the same means convincing, remembering that both 1 and 37 represent the physical constant of the hydrogen atom (1.370370370)—the basic absolute of all creation. Each of these numbers that represent the Elohim, when multiplied by 27 will also resolve to 27.

37   (37 x 27 = 999 resolves to 27)
37   *God,* אלהא, (Daniel 4:2)
37   *Only Son,* היחיד
37   *Power,* אול
370   *Everlasting righteousness,* צדק לעולם, (Psalm 119:142)
370   *He lives,* שכן, (Isaiah 33:5)
37   *Only begotten,* יחידה
370   *He rules,* משל, (Psalm 66:7)
370   *God (Elohim) is my King of old,* אלהים מלכי מקדם, (Psalm 74:12)

121

37   *Glory*, הכבוד
370   *Whole*, שלם
370   *Whole*, ολος
370   *God (Elohim)*, 86 + *God (Theos)* 284 = 370

37 x 2 = 74   (74 x 27 = 1998 resolves to 27)
74   *A great God*, אל גדול, (Psalm 95:3)
74   *Their Redeemer*, גאלם, (Jeremiah 50:34)
740   *Judge of all the earth*, השפט כל הארץ, (Genesis 18:25)
740   *Circle*, κυκλος
740   *Creation*, κτισις
74   *Foundation*, יסד
74   *Everlasting*, עד

37 x 3 = 111   (111 x 27 = 2997 resolves to 27)
111   *Wonderful*, אלפ, (Isaiah 9:6)
111   *The Most High*, עליא, (Daniel 4:32)
1110   *Only Son*, υιος μονος, (John 3:16)
1110   *The blood of Jesus*, το αιμα Ιησου, (I John 1:7)
111   *Son of the Living God*, בני אל חי, (Hosea 1:10)
111   *Lord of all*, אדון כל, (Zechariah 6:5)
111   *A precious stone*, אבן חן, (Proverbs 17:8)

37 x 4 = 148   (148 x 27 = 3996 resolves to 27)
1480   *Christ*, Χριστος
148   *The Most High*, אלהא עליא, (Daniel 4:2)
1480   *Son of God*, υιος Κυριος

37 x 5 = 185   (285 x 27 = 4995 resolves to 27)
185   *Rabbi*, ο ραββι
185   *Glory*, δοξαν
1850   *The Messiah, Word of the Father*, ο Μεσσιας Λογος
       Πατρος
1850   *The strong man* (representing Jesus), τον ισχυρον,
       (Matthew 12:29)

122

IN THE BEGINNING ELOHIM

37 x 6 = 222   (222 x 27 = 5994 resolves to 27)

222   *The Voice of God,* קול אלהים, (Deut. 4:33)

2220   *I am Alpha and Omega, εγω Αλφα και Ωμεγα*

222   *A stone of stumbling* (referring to Jesus as the topstone), ולאבן נגף, (Isaiah 8:14)

222   *The Lord is my Rock and my shield,* יהוה עזי ומגני, (Psalm 28:7)

222   *Nazarene, Ναζαρηνε*

2220   *Unto you that fear my name shall the Sun of Righteousness arise with healing in his wings,* ומרפא בכנפיה וזרחה לכם יראי שמי שמש צדקה, (Malachi 4:2)

37 x 7 = 259   (259 x 27 = 6993 resolves to 27)

259   *Kingdom, βασιλεια*

2590   *Only Son, Christ, υιος μονος Χριστος*

2590   *The seed of David* (referring to Jesus), *οτι εκ του σπερματος Δαυιδ,* (John 7:42)

37 x 8 = 296   (296 x 27 = 7992 resolves to 27)

296   *The Rock,* צור

296   *God,* צור

296   *Only begotten, μονογενη*

2960   *Son of Man, υιος του ανθρωπου,* (Matthew 8:20)

296   *Jehovah reigns forever,* יהוה ימלך לעלם, (Exodus 15:18)

296   *The mount of God (Elohim),* הר האלהים, (Exodus 18:5)

37 x 9 = 333   (333 x 27 = 8991 resolves to 27)

333   *Thy throne O God (Elohim) is forever,* כסאך אלהים עולם, (Psalm 45:6)

3330   *Lord of lords, Κυριος των κυριων*

3330   *The will of God in Christ Jesus, θελημα Θεου εν Χριστω Ιησου,* (I Thes. 5:18)

3330   *Behold I lay in Zion a chief cornerstone* (Jesus as the topstone of the Pyramid), *ιδου τιθημι εν Σιων λιθον ακρογωνιαιον,* (I Peter 2:6)

37 x 11 = 407   (407 x 27 = 10989 resolves to 27)
407   *Lord of all the earth,* אדון כל הארץ, ((Joshua 3:13)

37 x 12 = 444   (444 x 27 = 11988 resolves to 27)
4440   *The Lord Christ, τω Κυριω Χριστω,* (Col. 3:24)
4440   *Christ the Son of Man, Χριστος υιος του ανθρωπου*
444   *Atonement, καταλλαγην,* (Romans 5:11)
444   *The Rock of my refuge,* לצור מחסי, (Psalm 94:22)

37 x 13 = 481   (481 x 27 = 12987 resolves to 27)
481   *The beginning* (or genesis) of Christ, *η γενεσις,*
       (Matthew 1:1)

37 x 14 = 518   (518 x 27 = 13986 resolves to 27)
518   *Sun, ηλιου,* (Mark 16:2)
518   (I am) *the Door, η θυρα,* (John 10:9)
5180   *The stone which the builders rejected, the same is
       become the head of the corner, λιθον ον απεδοκιμασαν
       οι οικοδομουντες ουτος εγενηθη εις κεφαλην
       γωνιας,* (Luke 20:17)
5180   *The Father sent the Son to be the Saviour of the world,
       ο πατηρ απεσταλκεν τον υιον σωτηρα του κοσμου,*
       (I John 4:14)

37 x 15 = 555   (555 x 27 = 14985 resolves to 27)
5550   *Our Lord and his Christ, Κυριου ημων και του
       Χριστου αυτου,* (Revelation 11:15)
555   *Power, δυναμιν*

37 x 16 = 592   (592 x 27 = 15984 resolves to 27)
592   *Godhead, Θεοτης*
592   *The Lord of heaven,* מרא שמיא, (Daniel 5:23)
592   *Holiness, αγιοτης*
592   *The Holy One of Jacob,* קדוש יעקב, (Isaiah 29:23)

37 x 17 = 629   (629 x 27 = 16983 resolves to 27)
629   *The true Word, αληθης Λογος*

37 x 18 = 666   (666 x 27 = 17982 resolves to 27)
666   *The head of the corner*, ‏לראש פנה‎, (Psalm 118:22)
666   *Jehovah God that created the heavens*, ‏יהוה בורא השמים‎
     ‏האל‎, (Isaiah 42:5)
666   *He hath made the earth*, ‏עשה ארץ‎, (Jeremiah 10:12)
666   *Let there be lights*, ‏יהי מארת‎, (Genesis 1:14)

37 x 19 = 703   (703 x 27 = 18981 resolves to 27)
703   *The God of Israel, ο Θεος Ισραηλ*
703   *The Holy One of Israel, ο αγιοσ Ισραηλ*
703   *The God of David, Θεος Δαυιδ*

37 x 21 = 777   (777 x 27 = 20979 resolves to 27)
777   *The man child, τον αρσενα*, (Revelation 12:13)
777   *I* (Jehovah) *have raised him* (Jesus) *up*, ‏אנכי העירתהו‎,
     (Isaiah 45:13)

37 x 22 = 814   (814 x 27 = 21978 resolves to 27)
814   *The powerful Word* (of God), *ο λογος ενεργης,*
     (Hebrews 4:12)
814   *God, Θεω*, (Mark 10:27)
814   *His throne as the sun before me*, ‏כסאו כשמש נגדי‎, (Psalm
     89:36)

37 x 24 = 888   (888 x 27 = 23976 resolves to 27)
888   *Jesus, Ιησους*
888   *The Founder, ο οικιστης*
888   *I am the life, ειμι η ζωη*
888   *Thou Lord art exalted forever*, ‏אתה מרום לעלם יהוה‎,
     (Psalm 92:8)
888   *Salvation of our God*, ‏ישועת אלהינו‎, (Isaiah 52:10)

8880 *An ark, in which a few, that is eight souls were saved through water* (the ark pictured salvation through Jesus), κιβωτου εις ην ολιγοι τουτ εστιν οκτω ψυχαι διεσωθησαν δι υδατος, (I Peter 3:20)

8880 *Behold, a virgin shall conceive and bear a son, and they will call his name Emmanuel, which being interpreted is God with us,* ιδου η παρθενος εν γαστρι εξει και τεξεται υιον και καλεσουσιν ονομα αυτου Εμμανουηλ ο εστιν μεθερμηνευομενον μεθ ημων Θεος, (Matthew 1:23)

888 *I am Jehovah, I change not,* אני יהוה לא שניתי, (Malachi 3:6)

37 x 26 = 962 (962 x 27 = 25974 resolves to 27)
962 *Jehovah-shalom,* שלם, 370 x יהוה, 26 = 9620
962 *Godhead,* Θεοτητος, (Col. 2:9)
962 *Thou art clothed with honor and majesty,* והדר לבשת הוד, (Psalm 104:1)
962 *Forever O Lord thy Word is settled in heaven,* בשמים לעולם יהוה דברך נצב, (Psalm 119:89)

37 x 27 = 999 (999 x 27 = 26973 resolves to 27)
999 *In the beginning God (Elohim),* בראשית אלהים, (Genesis 1:1)
999 *Glory of God,* δοξαν Θεω, (Romans 4:20)
999 *A door of hope,* פתח תקוה, (Hosea 2:15)

37 x 28 = 1036 (1036 x 27 = 27972 resolves to 27)
1036 *God and the Lamb,* ο Θεος και το αρνιον (Rev. 21:23, *The glory of God did lighten it, and the Lamb is the light thereof.*)
1036 *I am the resurrection,* ειμι η αναστασις, (John 11:25)

37 x 29 = 1073 (1073 x 27 = 28971 resolves to 27)
1073 *The God of the earth,* ο Θεος της γης, (Genesis 24:3, Septuagint)

37 x 31 = 1147   (1147 x 27 = 30969 resolves to 27)
1147   *The will of God, θεληματος Θεου,* (Romans 15:32)

37 x 32 = 1184   (1184 x 27 = 31968 resolves to 27)
1184   *Chief cornerstone, ακρογωνιαιον,* (I Peter 2:6)
1184   *Throne of God, θρονου Θεου,* (Revelation 22:1)
1184   *In a different form, εν ετερα μορφη,* (Jesus, after his resurrection appeared *"in a different form"* to his disciples on the road to Emmaus), (Mark 16:12)

37 x 33 = 1221   (1221 x 27 = 32967 resolves to 27)
1221   *Wonderful, Θαυμαστος,* (the prophetic name of Jesus in Isaiah 9:6—Septuagint)
1221   *Carcase* (the humanity of Jesus as man's ransom price), *πτωμα,* (Matthew 24:28)
1221   *His feet shall stand in that day upon the Mount of Olives,* (prophetic of the return of Christ), על הר הזיתים עמדו רגליו ביום ההוא, (Zechariah 14:4)
1221   *Holy Master, δεσποτησ ο αγιος,* (Revelation 6:10)

37 x 36 = 1332   (1332 x 27 = 35964 resolves to 27)
1332   *Alpha, Omega* (first and last), *αλφα ω*
1332   *True God, αληθως Θεος*
1332   *Behold your King* (Jesus), *ιδου βασιλευς,* (John 12:15)

37 x 37 = 1369   1369 x 27 = 36963 resolves to 27)
1369   *Image of God, εικων Θεου,* (II Corinthians 4:4)
1369   *The God of life, ο Θεος ζωης*
1369   *The Son of David* (Jesus), *ο υιου Δαυιδ,* (Matthew 1:1)

37 x 39 = 1443   (1443 x 27 = 38961 resolves to 27)
1443   *The Word of the Lord, ο λογος Κυριου*
1443   *The peace of God, η ειρηνη του Θεου,* (Phil. 4:7)

37 x 42 = 1554 (1554 x 27 = 41958 resolves to 27)
1554 *Only Word of the Father, μονος λογος πατρος*
1554 *My beloved Son, υιον μου αγαπητον,* (Luke 10:13)
1554 *We have found the Messiah, ευρηκαμεν τον Μεσσιαν,* (John 1:41)

37 x 43 = 1591 (1591 x 27 = 42957 resolves to 27)
1591 *Spirit of life, πνευμα ζωης*
1591 *I am the Good Shepherd, εγω ειμι ο ποιμην ο καλος,* (John 10:11)

37 x 44 = 1628 (1628 x 27 = 43956 resolves to 9)
1628 *The head of the corner* (referring to Jesus as the topstone), *κεφαλη γωνιας,* (Matthew 21:42)
1628 *Son of David* (Jesus), *υιω Δαυιδ,* (Matthew 21:15)

37 x 45 = 1665 (1665 x 27 = 44955 resolves to 27)
1665 *The mouth of God, στοματος Θεου,* (Matthew 4:4)

37 x 46 = 1702 (1702 x 27 = 45954 resolves to 27)
1702 *Peace of the Father, ειρηνη του πατρος*
1702 *Jacob's well* (from which Jesus drank), *πηγη του Ιακωβ,* (John 4:6)

37 x 47 = 1739 (1739 x 27 = 45953 resolves to 27)
1739 *Christ Kingdom, Χριστος βασιλεια*

37 x 48 = 1776 (1776 x 27 = 47952 resolves to 27)
1776 *Lord of the sabbath, Κυριος σαββατου,* (Mark 2:28)
1776 *River of life, ποταμος ζωης,* (Revelation 22:1)
1776 (1778) *I came forth from the Father, εξηλθον εκ του πατρος,* (John 16:28)
1776 *The Lamb in the midst of the throne, οτι αρνιον ανα μεσον θρονου,* (Revelation 7:17)

37 x 49 = 1813   (1813 x 27 = 48951 resolves to 27)
1813   *Lord of hosts, Κυριος σαβαωθ,* (Septuagint)
1813   *Emmanuel, the Son of David, Εμμανουηλ ο υιος Δαυιδ*

37 x 51 = 1887   (1887 x 27 = 50949 resolves to 27)
1887   *The Father and the Son, τον πατερα και τον υιον,* (I John 2:22)
1887   *The One from heaven, εκ του ουρανου,* (John 3:13)

37 x 52 = 1924   (1924 x 27 = 51948 resolves to 27)
1924   *The God of the universe, ο Θεου του κοσμος*

37 x 53 = 1961   (1961 x 27 = 52947 resolves to 27)
1961   *The cornerstone, ο λιθος της γωνιας*

37 x 54 = 1998   (1998 x 27 = 53946 resolves to 27)
1998   *The son of the virgin, ο υιος εκ της παρθενου*
1998   *His only begotten Son, υιον αυτου μονογενη,* (I John 4:9)

37 x 55 = 2035   (2035 x 27 = 54945 resolves to 27)
2035   *Christ in you, Χριστος εν υμιν,* (Col. 1:27)
2035   *Wisdom of God* (used as a metaphor of Jesus), *σοφια του Θεου,* (Ephesians 3:10; I Cor. 1:24)
2035   *The righteousness of God* (used as a metaphor of Jesus), *η δικαιοσυνη του Θεου,* (II Pet. 1:1; Rom. 10:3)

37 x 56 = 2072   (2072 x 27 = 55944 resolves to 27)
2072   *The Alpha, the Omega* (the first, the last), *το αλφα το ω,* (Rev. 1:8)

37 x 57 = 2109   (2109 x 27 = 56943 resolves to 27)
2109   *Heir of the Kingdom of God, κληρονομος της*
        βασιλειας Θεου
2109   *He that sat upon the horse* (The King of kings and Lord
        of lords) *καθημενου επι του ιππου,* (Rev. 19:21)

37 x 59 = 2183   (2183 x 27 = 58941 resolves to 27)
2183   *The right hand of God, δεξιων του Θεου,* (Acts 7:55)
2183   *Christ the Holy One of Israel, Χριστος ο αγιος Ισραηλ*
2183   *Head over all things to the church* (referring to Jesus),
        κεφαλη υπερ παντα τη εκκλησια, (Eph. 1:22)

37 x 61 = 2257   (2257 x 27 = 60939 resolves to 27)
2257   *Gospel of Christ, ευαγγελιον Χριστου*
2257   *Noah's Ark* (an illustration of salvation through Christ),
        κιβωτος Νωε

37 x 62 = 2294   (2294 x 27 = 61938 resolves to 27)
2294   *His life* (Christ's), *τη ζωη αυτου,* (Rom. 5:10)

37 x 63 = 2331   (2331 x 27 = 62937 resolves to 27)
2331   *This Jesus hath God raised up, τον Ιησουν ανεστησεν*
        ο Θεος, (Acts 2:32)

37 x 64 = 2368   (2368 x 27 = 63936 resolves to 27)
2368   *Jesus Christ* (it can be spelled *Ιησους Χριστος* or *Ιησου*
        Χριστου, depending on its placement in the sentence,
        but it still adds to 2368)
2368   *Him for whom are all things* (Jesus), *αυτω δι ον τα*
        παντα, (Heb. 2:10)

37 x 66 = 2442   (2442 x 27 = 65934 resolves to 27)
2442   *The Son of God, τη υιου του Θεου,* (Gal. 2:20)
2442   *Jesus, the name given by the angel, Ιησους το κληθεν*
        υπο αγγελου, (Luke 2:21)

37 x 69 = 2553   (2553 x 27 = 68931 resolves to 27)

2553   *Name of the only begotten Son of God, ονομα*
μονογενους υιου Θεου, (John 3:18)

37 x 72 = 2664   (2664 x 27 = 71928 resolves to 27)

2664   *The Lord God is one Lord, Κυριος Θεος εις εστιν,*
κυριος, (Mark 12:29)

37 x 73 = 2701   (2701 x 27 = 72927 resolves to 27)

2701   *The grace of Christ, χαριτι Χριστου,* (Gal. 1:6)

2701   *In the beginning God created the heaven and the earth,*
בראשית אלהים ברא את השמים ואת הארץ(Gen. 1:1)

37 x 75 = 2775   (2775 x 27 = 74925 resolves to 27)

2775   *The Prince of Life* (Jesus), *τον αρχηγον της ζωης,*
(Acts 3:15)

37 x 76 = 2812   (2812 x 27 = 75924 resolves to 27)

2812   *His eternal power and Godhead, η αιδιος αυτου*
δυναμις και Θειοτης, (Rom. 1:20)

2812   *Blood of Christ, αιματι του Χριστου,* (Eph. 2:13)

2812   *Eternal redemption, αιωνιαν λυτρωσιν,* (Heb. 9:12)

37 x 85 = 3145   (3145 x 27 = 84915 resolves to 27)

3145   *Lord of heaven and earth, Κυριε του ουρανου και*
της γης, (Luke 10:21)

37 x 86 = 3182   (3182 x 27 = 85914 resolves to 27)

3182   *The Lion of the tribe of Judah* (Jesus), *ο λεων ο εκ της*
φυλης Ιουδα, (Rev. 5:5)

37 x 91 = 3367   (3367 x 27 = 90909 resolves to 27)

3367   *Father of spirits, πατρι των πνευματων,* (Heb. 12:9)

37 x 92 = 3404   (3404 x 27 = 91908 resolves to 27)
3404   *His divine power, της θειας δυναμεως αυτου,* (II Pet. 1:3)

37 x 93 = 3441   (3441 x 27 = 92907 resolves to 27)
3441   *The riches of His glory, τον πλουτον της δοξης αυτου,* (Rom. 9:23)
3441   *A High Priest after the order of Melchizedek* (Jesus), *αρχιερευς κατα την ταξιν Μελχισεδεκ,* (Heb. 5:10)

37 x 95 = 3515   (3515 x 27 = 94905 resolves to 27)
3515   *The spirit of Jesus Christ, πνευματος Ιησου Χριστου,* (Phil 1:19)

37 x 96 = 3552   (3552 x 27 = 95904 resolves to 27)
3552   *Author of eternal salvation, αιτιος σωτηριας αιωνιου,* (Heb. 5:9)
3552   *The mystery of God, του μυστηριου του Θεου,* (Col. 2:2)

37 x 98 = 3626   (3626 x 27 = 97902 resolves to 27)
3626   *This is my body* (Christ's), *τουτο εστιν το σωμα μου,* (Matt. 26:26)

37 x 101 = 3737   (3737 x 27 = 100899 resolves to 27)
3737   *Jesus Christ the son of David, Ιησου Χριστου ο υιου Δαυιδ,* (Matt. 1:1)
3737   *The God of our fathers, ο Θεος των πατερων ημων,* (Acts 22:14)

37 x 102 = 3774   (3774 x 27 = 101898 resolves to 27)
3774   *The Messiah, the Saviour of the world, ο Μεσσιας ο σωτηρ του κοσμου*
3774   *The God of heaven, τω Θεω του ουρανου,* (Rev. 11:13)

37 x 103 = 3811   (3811 x 27 = 102897 resolves to 27)
3811   *The person of Christ,* προσωπω Χριστου, (II Cor. 2:10)

37 x 109 = 4033   (4033 x 27 = 108891 resolves to 27)
4033   *The firstborn of all creation,* πρωτοτοκος πασης κτισεως, (Col. 1:15)

37 x 115 = 4255   (4255 x 27 = 114885 resolves to 27)
4255   *The firstborn from the dead,* (the resurrected Jesus), ο πρωτοτοκος των νεκρων, (Rev. 1:5)

37 x 122 = 4551   (4551 x 27 = 122877 resolves to 27)
4551   *Jesus standing on the right hand of God,* Ιησουν εστωτα εκ δεξιων του Θεου, (Acts 7:55)

37 x 124 = 4588   (4588 x 27 = 123876 resolves to 27)
4588   *The Prince of the kings of the earth* (Jesus), ο αρχων των βασιλεων της γης, (Rev. 1:5)

37 x 131 = 4847   (4847 x 27 = 130869 resolves to 27)
4847   *God, who quickeneth all things,* του Θεου του ζωογονουν τος τα παντα, (I Tim. 6:13)

37 x 144 = 5328   (5328 x 27 = 143856 resolves to 27)
5328   (5330) *The right hand of the throne of the Majesty in the heavens,* δεξια του θρονου της μεγαλωσυνης εν τοις ουρανιος, (Heb. 8:1)
37 x 223 = 8251   (8251 x 27 = 222777 resolves to 27)
8251   *In him was life, and the life was the light of men,* εν αυτω ζωη ην, και η ζωη ην το φως των ανθρωπων, (John 1:4)

The list is impressive, but by no means exhaustive.

The number 37 is a prime—that is, it is only divisible by 1. How interesting to note that each of the digits, when raised to its triplet, its highest concept, is divisible by 37—and this in increments of 3, thus:

```
 1 x 37 =  37
 3 x 37 = 111
 6 x 37 = 222
 9 x 37 = 333
12 x 37 = 444
15 x 37 = 555
18 x 37 = 666
21 x 37 = 777
24 x 37 = 888
+27 x 37 = 999
```

136 = *I am Jehovah, the first and the last,* ואת אחרנים
אני יהוה ראשון, (Isaiah 41:4)

136 = *The right hand of Jehovah,* ימין יהוה,
(Psalm 118:16)

As already noted in chapter 4, the cubic volume of the Great Pyramid is 37,000,000 cubic feet. The mean of earth's orbit around the sun is 186 million miles in diameter, making a circumference of 584.336 million miles. If this distance were stated in inches, it would be 37 with many zeros after it.

The relationship of the number 37 to 27 is of utmost significance because it has to do with the beginning of things, with the sun, with light and with the Elohim. The speed of light is 186,000 miles per second. If this were measured by the reed it would be 93,000. If 93 were divided by the common denominator of 27, the result would be 3.44 (93 ÷ 27 = 3.44), and the number 344 is the gematria for *"the light of the world,"* το φως του κοσμου, (Matt. 5:14). Its connection with the Pyramid is in the gematria for *"great wonder,"* μεγαλα σημεια, 344. If 344 were the diameter of a circle, the circumference would be 1080—a number full of meaning.

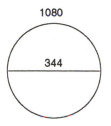

1080   *God himself that formed the earth and made it,* האָרץ ועשׂה
        הוא האלהים יצר, (Isaiah 45:18)

1080   *The Lord is in His holy temple, let all the earth keep*
        silence before Him, יהוה בהיכל קדשׁו הסמפניו כל הארץ, (Hab.
        2:20)

1080   *Heaven is my throne and the earth is my footstool,* רגלי
        השׁמים כסאי והארץ הדם, (Isaiah 66:1)

The solar and lunar numbers, when added, become 1080
(864 + 216 = 1080).

The hydrogen atom has an atomic weight of 1.008. In all
these numbers, the zeros can be deleted for purposes of gematria,
giving the basic number of 18, which is the number equivalent
of the Biblical name for the Creator—*Maker,* פעל, 180.[1]

The number 1080 is shown in the relationship of Jesus to
the sun. The number 8 represents a new beginning through
Jesus (*Jesus,* 888). Multiply 1080 by 8 and the product is 8640,
the solar number. Similarly, if we multiply 8 by 27, the number
for light, the product is 216, the lunar number. And, to complete the picture, if we multiply 99 *(the garden of the Lord)* by
8, the product is 792, the earth number. The three computations
are as follows:

1080 x 8 = 8640 — Diameter of the sun 864,000 miles
  27 x 8 = 216 — Diameter of the moon 2,160 miles
  99 x 8 = 792 — Diameter of the earth 7,920 miles

1 The walls of the King's Chamber in the Great Pyramid contain 100 granite
blocks: 37 south wall; 27 north wall; 18 east wall; 18 west wall. (The first four
courses contain 93; the fifth course contains 7, totalling 100.)

The relationship of the Elohim to the sun can be shown by simple addition. In the creation verses of Genesis 1, the exclamation *"Let there be light,"* יהי אור, has a number value of 232. The gematria for *Elohim*, אלהים, is 86. Add these together and they give the gematria for the *sun*, ηλιος, 318.

> 86   *Elohim*
> <u>232</u>   *Let there be light*
> 318   *Sun*

> 318 x π = 999   *In the beginning Elohim*

Light from the sun provides the active ingredients for all life on earth. Plants transform this light into food for growth through the process of photosynthesis, only because the carbon, hydrogen, nitrogen and magnesium in the chlorophyll molecule are arranged in a symmetrical pattern of twelve. This twelve-fold symmetry is the life-giver that transforms light into organic substance.

The atomic numbers of the four elements necessary for photosynthesis are:

> carbon   6
> hydrogen   1
> nitrogen   7
> magnesium   <u>12</u>
>   26 = *Jehovah*, יהוה

A student of the Bible soon realizes that the number 12 is a basic foundation number. There are so many twelves mentioned in scripture it cannot be overlooked. Yet the word *foundation,* יסד, bears the number 74. In Psalm 102:25, we are told *"Thou hast laid the foundations of the earth,"* הארץ יסדת, which adds to 740. But look at what happens when we multiply or add these two foundation numbers.

IN THE BEGINNING ELOHIM

$$12 \times 74 = 888 \quad \textit{Jesus, } I\eta\sigma o\upsilon\varsigma$$
$$12 + 74 = 86 \quad \textit{Elohim, } \text{אלהים}$$

These two foundation numbers are telling us *"In the beginning Elohim created the heaven and the earth, "* (Genesis 1:1).[1]

The word *"geometry"* means "measure of the earth." It is the study of spatial order through the measure and relationships of forms. The three basic geometric figures that define spatial order are the circle, square and triangle.

Ancient geometry began with *One*, which, as we have shown, represents the El and its first division into the Elohim. Today our geometry begins with *zero;* however, this is of relatively modern invention, coming into use about the eighth century A.D. The invention of zero permitted numbers to represent ideas which have no form. From the point of view of the natural world, zero does not exist; it is a completely mental entity. Science today shows us a continual fluctuation and alternation between matter and energy ($E=mc^2$), confirming that in the natural world there is no zero.

Robert Lawlor stated it simply and succinctly:

> We have had to learn that there is nowhere that we can dispose of the things we have finished using—that there is no zero drain in our sink; there is no factory pipe or hole in the ground that does not lead somewhere. Everything remains here with us; the cycles of growth, utilization and decay are unbroken. There is no throwaway bottle. With zero we have at the beginning of

---

1 The gematria for *Elohim,* אלהים, is 86. The factors of 86 are 1, 2, and 43; making the sum of the factors 46. The gematria for *number* in Hebrew, מני, is 100; the gematria for *substance* in Hebrew, עצמ, is 200; and the gematria for *number in* Greek, $\alpha\rho\iota\theta\mu o\varsigma$, is 430. Number and substance are interchangeable, and are basic factors of the Elohim. The sum of these factors, is 46, the gematria of the Hebrew word for *measure,* אמה, which is a unit of number and substance.

modern mathematics a number concept which is philo-
sophically misleading and one which creates a separa-
tion between our system of numerical symbols and the
structure of the natural world. On the other hand, with
the notion of Unity, which governs ancient mathematics,
there is no such dichotomy.[1]

A circle is a perfect illustration of Unity, having no beginning
nor ending; but a beautiful pattern emerges when we draw a
circle, then build another identical circle whose circumference
passes through the center of the beginning circle. The circle is
thus projected outward in a perfect reflection of itself.

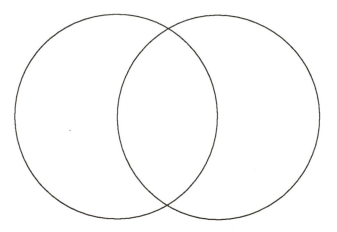

One circle becomes two by division—the second becomes
the image of the first—the El becoming the Elohim. This was
the active principle in the creation of matter. If the hydrogen
atom, with its one proton, represents the El, then the hydrogen
molecule, which is the division of one into two, represents the

---

1   Robert Lawlor, *Sacred Geometry,* The Crossroads Publishing Co., New
York, NY, 1982, page 20.

Elohim. It is the fusion of the two atoms in the hydrogen molecule that creates the massive amounts of heat and light which comes from the sun. The fusion, or the Unity of the Father and Son, become the one source of all creation.

This principle of division was the active principle in the creation of all matter. Each of the elements of which all matter is composed is identified by the number of protons in its nucleus—all divisions of, and consequently exact replicas of the one in the hydrogen atom.

Understanding this principle, physicists have "created" many new elements, by adding more protons to the atoms of the existing elements. They have, in fact, not "created" anything. They have more properly "re-arranged" the replicas of the first real creation, which was the one proton in the hydrogen atom.

The two interlocking circles which represent the fusion of the Elohim, do, in fact, create a third figure which is common to both. It is known as the Vesica. These overlapping circles represent Unity in the midst of becoming dual—or to be more specific, the El becoming the Elohim. In Colossians 1:15 we are told he is *"the image of the invisible God, the firstborn of every creature."* The Vesica that is formed by this "growth by division" was used by early Christians as the symbol of Christ— the fish. Thus it has been named the Vesica Piscis.

The *sign* of the fish is still used by Christians today. The word "fish" in Greek is *Icthus, Ιχθυς,* 1219, which was used as an acronym for *Jesus Christ, Son of God, Saviour.*[1]

The gematria for the *sign* of the fish, *Icthus,* beautifully shows its inter-relationship with the *signs* previously mentioned. If *Icthus, Ιχθυς,* 1219, were the circumference of a circle, the diameter would be 388—a number that beautifully represents both Father and Son, the sun, and the topstone.

---

1 St. Augustine's book 18 of *The City of God* is acrostic, and the first letter of each line forms the words ΙΗΣΟΥΣ ΧΡΙΣΤΟΣ ΘΕΟΥ ΥΙΟΣ ΣΩΤΗΡ, Jesus Christ, Son of God, Saviour—and the acrostic of this is ΙΧΘΥΣ, the fish.

388   *One God, γαρ Θεος,* (I Tim. 2:5)
3880   *The Revelation of Jesus Christ, αποκαλυψις Ιησου Χριστου,* (Rev. 1:1)
3880   *The throne of His father David* (speaking prophetically of the kingship of Jesus), *τον θρονον Δαυιδ του πατρος αυτου,* (Luke 1:32)
388   *The sun, ο ηλιος,* (Rev. 6:12)
388   *Rock,* חלמיש,

The overlapping circles, forming the Vesica Piscis, is the projection of the circle outward in a perfect reflection of itself, *"The firstborn of every creature."* Thus the El has become the Elohim.

We saw the unmistakable evidence that the number 37 is the prime that represents this Unity. How fitting that the Hebrew word כדגי, which, when translated into English, means *"like a fish,"* has a number equivalent of 37.

If 37 were the width of the Vesica Piscis, it would also be the radius of each circle, making the total width 3 x 37 = 111. The beautiful relationship of 111 to the Elohim has been shown on page 115. The diameter of each circle would be 74, the gematria of which is shown on page 122. The number 74, as shown, not only relates to the Elohim but also to a *circle, κυκλος,* 740; *foundation,* יסד, 74; *creation, κτισις,* 740; and *everlasting,* עד, 74. The number 74, the diameter of each of these circles, speaks loudly and clearly of the basic fundamentals of creation as are embodied in the Elohim.

The circumference of each of these circles is 232—a number relating to the Elohim and to creation. Note its gematria below:

232   *Jehovah has spoken,* יהוה דבר, (Isa. 1:2)
232   *The Word of the Lord,* דבר יהוה, (Isa. 1:10)
232   *Let there be light,* יהי אור, (Gen. 1:3)

Modern science and astronomy speak of the "Big Bang" theory of creation. Could this be more accurately defined as a

140

"sonic boom" from the Voice of God? In Hebrews 11:3 we are told, *"The worlds were framed by the Word of God."* And in II Peter 3:5 it states, *"by the Word of God the heavens were of old."* Peter was quoting Psalm 33:6: *"By the Word of the Lord were the heavens made, and all the host of them by the breath of his mouth."* Robert Lawlor, in *Sacred Geometry,* states it thus:

> This clearly restates the ancient image of universal creation through sound waves or the Word of God; science reaffirms that visible stars and galaxies are spiral blast patterns, residual imprints of standing shock waves from the thundering voice of the Universe."

The vesica formed by the two overlapping circles has a height of 64 and a width of 37. Subtract, and the difference between height and width is 27, the common denominator of light. Multiply the two figures and the product is 2368, the gematria for Jesus Christ, (64 x 37 = 2368, *Jesus Christ, Ιησους Χριστος,* 2368). It is the man Jesus that is represented by the Vesica Piscis. The number 64 is the gematria for *truth, αληθεια;* and surely he was the personification of truth.

The Hebrew word for *fish* is דאג, which has a number value of 8—the number that represents a new life through Jesus. It is fitting that 8 x 8 = 64, the height of the Vesica Piscis.

The perimeter of the vesica is 155. The gematria for *the Christ, ο Χριστος,* is 1550. As the Word, he was also the *first, πρωτος,* 1550.

The proportional dimension of the cross can be inscribed within the vesica. It would have a height of 64 and a cross beam of 29.6. The *only begotten, μονογενη,* has a number equivalent of 296, as does *Son of Man, υιος του ανθρωπου,* (2960). It was the only begotten of the Father who hung upon that cross, in a human body, a son of man. I do not think it a coincidence that 8 (*fish,* דאג) times 296 is 2368, the gematria for Jesus Christ.

No records are available giving the dimensions of the cross upon which Jesus was crucified. William Stirling, in *The Canon* (pages 144-147) gives evidence for a cross proportion of 28 to 13, or more accurately 28 to 12.95. This would be, in whole numbers, 80 to 37. Because the number 8, as well as the number 37, so profoundly represent the man who hung on that cross, it seems probable that this was indeed the correct proportion. It makes a high upright in proportion to the crossbeam, but it must be remembered that a sufficient proportion would have

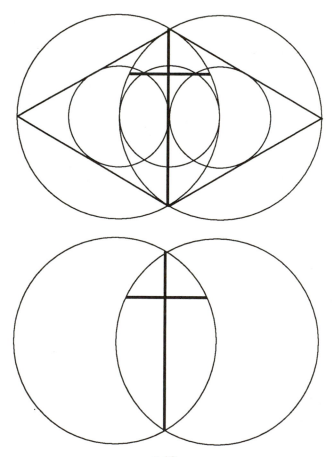

been into the ground to make it stable. These proportions precisely fit the geometrical progressions of the Vesica Piscis.

A rhombus inscribed within the vesica would have a perimeter of 148.

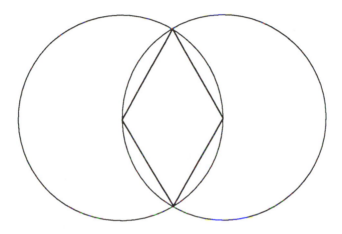

In keeping with the meaning of this *sign* of the fish—Jesus Christ, Son of God, Saviour— we find the number 1480 to be the gematria for the title, *Christ, Χριστος,* as well as the number for *Son of God, υιος Κυριος,* 1480. The number for *Saviour, σωτηρ,* is 1408. The same number, 148, is thus used for all three parts of the title from which the acronym Icthus is taken. (In gematria, zeros may be deleted as they are simply place holders).

Each side of the vesica is one-third of each circle, thus the height of the vesica forms one side of an equilateral triangle that can be inscribed within each circle.

The height of the vesica is 64, therefore the perimeter of the equilateral triangle is 3 x 64 = 192, a number that is used in scripture to describe both the Father and the Son.

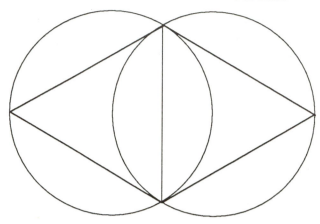

192   *The everlasting God,* אלהי עולם, (Isa. 40:28)
192   *The Lord Most High,* יהוה עליץ, (Psalm 47:2)
1920   *He is God* (Elohim) *in the heavens above and on the*
        earth below, הוא אלהים בשמים ממעל ועל הארץ מתחת,
        (Joshua 1:11)
1920   *The Lord of glory* (Jesus), *τον Κυριον της δοξης,*
        (I Cor. 2:8)

Putting it all together, the pattern looks like this:

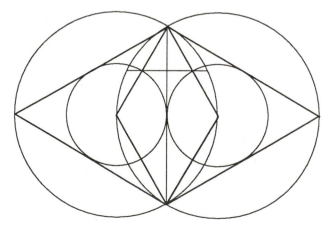

IN THE BEGINNING ELOHIM

When viewing the complete pattern, it becomes obvious that the proportions of the cross fit geometrically, thus becoming a part of the harmonious whole

Notice that circles can be inscribed within the equilateral triangles, using the same centers as the large circles. We will call the large circles the outer pattern, and the smaller circles the inner pattern. Both are identical except the inner pattern is exactly half the size of the outer pattern. Below is a demonstration of the gematria of these two patterns, based on the number 37 being the width of the Vesica Piscis.

Outer pattern:

Circumference of circle	232
Diameter of circle	74
Height of vesica (and cross)	64
Width of vesica	37
Perimeter of vesica	155
Crossbeam of cross	29.6
Perimeter of rhombus	148
Perimeter of triangle	192

Inner pattern:

Circumference of circle	116
Diameter of circle	37
Height of vesica (and cross)	32
Width of vesica	18.5
One side of vesica	38.8
Crossbeam of cross	14.8
Perimeter of rhombus	74
Perimeter of triangle	96

The relationship of the numbers in the outer pattern to the gematria of the scriptures has been shown above. The gematria for the inner pattern is as follows:

116   *Jehovah is King,* יהוה מלך, (Psalm 10:16)
116   *His right hand* (the position of authority given to Jesus), ימינו, (Isaiah 62:8)
116   *The mouth of the Lord* (the Word), פי יהוה, (Isa. 1:20)
116   *The Lord reigneth,* יהוה מלך, (Psalm 93:1)

37   (has been shown)

32   *His glory,* כבדו, (Deut. 5:24)
32   *Only Son,* יחיד
3200   *The Majesty in the Heaven,* της μεγαλωσυνης εν ουρανοις, (Hebrews 8:1)

185   *Rabbi* (the Master), ο ραββι
1850   *The strong man* (representing Jesus), τον ισχυρον, (Matt. 12:29)
1850   *The Messiah, Word of the Father,* ο μεσσιας λογος πατρος

388   *One God,* γαρ Θεος, (I Tim. 2:5)

148   (has been shown)

74   (has been shown)

96   *His mouth* (the Word of creation), פיו, (Psalm 33:6)
960   *Gift* (of God—Jesus), δωρεαν, (John 4:10)
960   *I am the Great King says the Lord of Hosts,* יהוה צבאות מלך גדול אני אמר, (Mal. 1:14)

The two overlapping circles, forming the vesica, represent the Father and the Son—the Son being the exact image of the Father. Within these two circles and their vesica, the proportions of the Great Pyramid can be drawn, using the radius of the circle (37) as the sides, and the center of each circle as the apex.

Eight such pyramids will precisely fit in the overlapping circles.

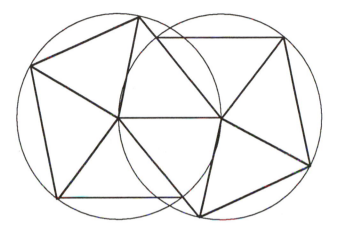

These pyramids will each have sides of 37, a base of 45.7 and a height of 29. The complete pyramid configuration has a perimeter of 288. These numbers continue to tell the same story. The number 457 is the gematria for *"God, the Holy One,"* והאל הקדש, while *"My righteous servant,"* (meaning Jesus), עבדי צדיק, (Isaiah 53:11), has a number equivalent of 290. The complete pyramid configuration is enclosed within a perimeter of 288, the gematria for *"Kingdom of heaven,"* βασιλεια των ουρανων. All that is contained within the Great Pyramid pertains to God's great plan for the establishing and completion of the Kingdom of Heaven. It is the *sign* and the *witness* in the land of Egypt.

The square base of that Pyramid, at its socket level, had sides of 365.242 Pyramid cubits—the number of days in the solar tropical year, or the number of revolutions of the earth in one orbit of the sun. The Great Pyramid was known as *"the light,"* and if we were to consider its square base as the squaring of the speed of light, the basic denominator in the formula for creation, each side of the Pyramid would represent 8649. Divide that number by the actual side measure of 365.242, and the result will be 23.68, the number for the name Jesus Christ.

186 x 186 = 34596
34596 ÷ 4 = 8649
8649 ÷ 365.242 = 23.68, Jesus Christ

square
base of
Great Pyramid

8649 ÷ 365.242

Before leaving this chapter—In The Beginning Elohim—let's look back, for a moment, to the creation of our solar system, and the measurement of its substance. According to the 1990 figures published by NASA, the diameters of the planets are as follows.

Mercury	3,032
Venus	7,519
Earth	7,926[1]
Mars	4,194
Jupiter	88,736
Saturn	74,978
Uranus	32,193
Neptune	30,775
Pluto	1,423

1 This figure is usually rounded to 7,920 for use in most computations.

The total miles, if all were added together, would be 250,776. Thus 9 planets would be represented by the division by 9, giving 27,864 miles for each, (250,776 ÷ 9 = 27,864). This is exciting because 27 is the common denominator of light, and 864 is the solar number, the source of light. The number 27,864 resolves to 27. If we divided this average of the planets by 27, the result would be 1032 (27,864 ÷ 27 = 1032), a number that relates to visible light—*white,* לבנים, 132.

If we multiplied the number for *Elohim,* אלהים, 86, by the foundation number, 12 (foundation, מוסדי, 120), the product would be 1032 (86 x 12 = 1032).

When we add the diameter of the sun, the center of the solar system, to the aggregate of the planets, the total measure of substance is 1,114,776, (864,000 + 250,776 = 1,114,776). If we again obtained an average, dividing by 10, the measure for each would be represented by the number 111,477.6. This number resolves to 27. If we divided it by 27, the common denominator for light, the result would be 4128.8. The number 4128 is the number of years from the first Adam to the second Adam; and the number 8 represents the second Adam (Jesus) and a new beginning. The apostle John called him *"the Lamb slain from the foundation of the world,"* and truly it was the plan from the beginning, before the worlds were made.

The Lord (Jehovah) possessed me in the beginning of his way, before his works of old. I was set up from everlasting, from the beginning, or ever the earth was. When there were no depths, I was brought forth; when there were no fountains abounding with water. Before the mountains were settled, before the hills was I brought forth: while as yet he had not made the earth, nor the fields, nor the highest part of the dust of the world. When he prepared the heavens, I was there: when he set a compass upon the face of the depth; when he established the clouds above; when he strengthened the fountains of the deep; when he gave to the sea his

*decree that the waters should not pass his command-
ment: when he appointed the foundations of the earth:
then I was by his side, like a master workman; and I was
daily his delight, rejoicing always before him; rejoicing in the world, his earth, and my delights were with
the sons of men.* (Proverb 8:22-31)

What a beautiful description of the relationship of the
Elohim, the Father and the Son, from the beginning. The son
took delight in the *"sons of men"* because he knew he would
come to earth to die for them, to be their Redeemer. It was an
act of love!

Waiting for the sunrise at Stonehenge

150

6
The Sign of the Rainbow

"Behold, I, even I, am establishing my covenant with you, and with your seed after you, and with every living creature which is with you.... And I have established my covenant with you, and all flesh shall not be cut off again by the waters of the flood; nor shall there ever again be a flood to destroy the earth. And God (Elohim) said, This is the sign of the covenant which I am about to make between me and you, and every living soul which is with you, for everlasting generations; I have set my bow in the cloud, and it shall be a sign of a covenant between me and the earth. And when I gather clouds on the earth, then the bow shall be seen in the clouds.... And God (Elohim) said to Noah, this is the sign of the covenant which I have established between me and all flesh that is on the earth."

The sign of the covenant was a beautiful rainbow, emblazoned across the sky, displaying all of the colors of the spectrum, and reaching down and touching the earth.

This beautiful display of light came at the end of an awesome experience. Noah had been in the ark for 370 days; part of that time drifting, he knew not where, through torrents, and currents that made his box-shaped vessel toss aimlessly. Finally it came to rest on a mountain, and as the waters of the flood receded, he and his family emerged out onto an earth that had been stripped of all life, both man and beast.

151

The story is not a myth. The great flood catastrophe really did happen. The evidences it has left in the earth are there to verify the fact. But it is more than just an event in the ancient history of man.

The Ark was the means of salvation for Noah and his family. All who were not in the Ark perished in the flood. The Ark is a fitting illustration of the means of salvation which is Jesus Christ. Many evidences of this relationship make the concept apparent.

Noah and his family were in the ark 370 days. The number 370, as has been shown, relates to Jesus Christ. If we were to state those 370 days as hours, it would be 8880 (370 x 24 = 8880). The gematria for the name *Jesus, Ιησους,* is 888. But the intended relationship becomes obvious when we look at the statement made by the Apostle Peter (I Peter 3:20): *"An Ark, in which a few, that is, eight souls were saved by water,"* κιβωτου εις ην ολιγοι τουτ εστιν οκτω ψυχαι διεσωθησαν δι υδατος, which has a number equivalent of 8880. The Ark was the means of salvation for those eight persons, just as Jesus Christ is the means of salvation for all mankind. It is fitting that *"the salvation of our God,"* ישועת אלהינו, (Isaiah 52:10) also has a number equivalent of 888—a prophecy concerning Jesus as representing salvation.

The dimensions of the Ark were 300 cubits long, by 50 cubits wide, by 30 cubits high—a long narrow box. The proportion of width to length was 1 to 6. This proportion can be overlaid on the two overlapping circles that form the vesica with precision. It appears to become a part of the intended pattern. Using the vesica with the width of 37, the dimensions of the ark become 18.5 by 111, and we have seen in chapter 5 the relationship of these numbers to Jesus.

To obtain the actual dimensions of the Ark, it is first necessary to find the length of the cubit that was used. Rev. John McClintock, D.D., and James Strong, S.T.D. in their *Cyclopaedia of Biblical, Theological and Ecclesiastical Literature,* Vol. VII, p. 147, suggest a cubit of 21 inches for the

THE SIGN OF THE RAINBOW

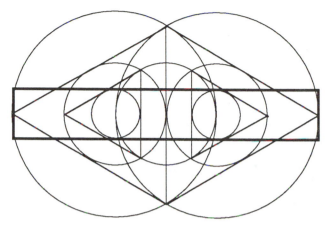

Ark. This is a fraction shorter than the great cubit that God gave to Ezekiel, which was 21.12 inches. If the great cubit is indeed the correct one, it is evidence for the antiquity of the British mile unit, for the length of the Ark would be exactly the 10th part of a mile, or 528 feet. The height would be the 100th part of a mile, or 52.8 feet. The width would bear the number that represents salvation through Jesus Christ, 88 feet. It is likely that this was indeed the unit used, for evidence has been shown that the great cubit played an important role in the construction of the Great Pyramid, built 333 years after, and of Stonehenge, built 500 years after.

The promise that God gave to Noah, *"I will establish my covenant,"* והקמתי אתבריתי, has a number value of 1584. A square with sides of 1584 has a perimeter of 6336, which is the number of inches in the length of the Ark.

If the cubit used to measure the Ark is indeed the great cubit, the width of the Ark in British inches would be 1,056, the length of the reed (10.56 feet), as well as the length of each of the lintels that topped the Sarsen Circle at Stonehenge (10.56 feet). The number 1056 relates to Noah, for his birth was in 1056 A.M. *(Anno Mundi),* or 1056 years from the creation of Adam.

153

The length of the Ark was six times its width. Thus the geometric proportion of its floor is six squares of 88 feet per side. Each square measures 352 feet in perimeter, and when multiplied by 6, gives a total of 2,112. The number not only defines the length of the great cubit, it also points to the one who came to provide salvation for man. *"A virgin shall conceive and bear a son and shall call his name Immanuel,"* אל העלמה הרה וילדת בן וקר את שמו עמנו, 2112, (Isaiah 7:14).

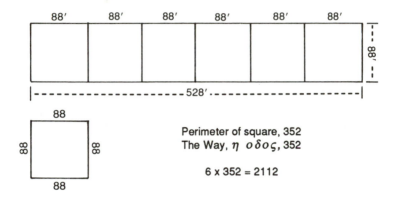

88' 88' 88' 88' 88' 88'

88'

|— — — — — — — — — — — — — — — 528' — — — — — — — — — — — — — —|

88
88   88
88

Perimeter of square, 352
The Way, η οδος, 352

6 x 352 = 2112

At the end of the 370 days in the Ark, Noah and his family, 8 persons, emerged from the Ark into a silent world. Every living creature had been destroyed by the flood of waters. The sky was beginning to clear, and the sunlight shone upon the misty sky, forming the huge arc of a rainbow. It was the *sign* that a covenant had been made—a promise by God that never again would he cause a flood to destroy the earth. The *sign* was light—light from the sun, which was refracted from the tiny drops of rain in the air, breaking the light into its spectrum of color. From the stance of the viewer, this bow of color formed the half of a circle, reaching from the sky to the ground, a full 180°. If we were to multiply the 180° by the length of the cubit, 1.76, the product would be 316.8, the same as the name *Lord Jesus Christ, Κυριος Ιησους Χριστος,* 3168.

THE SIGN OF THE RAINBOW

The Hebrew word for *bow*, קשת, means "bending," and bears the number 800. In the New Testament the word for *rainbow* is ιρις, 320. Multiply them (8 x 32) and the product is 256, which is one side of a square whose perimeter is 1024. In Genesis we are told that the rainbow was *"the sign of the covenant,"* אות הברית, 1024.

The use of the numbers 8 and 32 in the description of the rainbow is significant, because these are the two numbers, when multiplied by light (27), that produce the solar and lunar numbers.

$$32 \times 27 = 864$$
$$8 \times 27 = 216$$

This connection with the light from the sun is shown also at Stonehenge by the alignment of the summer solstice sunrise, which forms the axis of the monument, for the distance from the center to the base of the Heelstone is precisely 256 feet—it points directly to the sun on the morning of the summer solstice.

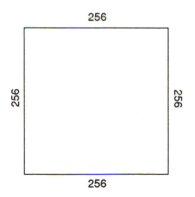

256

256

256

256

Perimeter 1024
The sign of the covenant, 1024

The same number was used for that other *"sign"*—the Great Pyramid. *"An altar and a pillar to Jehovah,"* מזבח ומצבה ליהוה, has a number value of 256 (Isaiah 19:19).

In Hebrew, the idea of *"to give light,"* נור, also has the number value of 256.

Another ark, or box, out from which shone the Shechinah light, was the ark in the Tabernacle, הארן, which also bears the number 256.

The rainbow that reached across the sky was a beautiful sight to behold—a display of the colors of visible light. It was actually a complete circle of color; however, those who observed it were only able to see the top half; the bottom half was below the horizon. The colors were arranged in the order of the spectrum—red at the top, followed by orange, yellow, green, blue and violet.

Each of the colors of visible light are determined by the length of the light wave. The units commonly used for this measurement are the *millimicron,* which is denoted by the sumbol $\mu\mu$, which equals one millionth of a millimeter; and the Angstrom unit (A. U.), which is one ten millionth of a millimeter.

Since it has been observed that the sacred numbers and measures do not use the metric system, the table below converts these units into the British inch.[1]

	$\mu\mu$	A. U.	Inch
Red	710	7,100	.00000284
Orange	620	6,200	.00000248
Yellow	570	5,700	.00000228
Green	520	5,200	.00000208
Blue	470	4,700	.00000188
Violet	410	4,100	.00000164
	aggregate		.00001320

---

1 The numbers given in the table are the wave lengths through the center of each color range, giving the truest color.

When the colors of the spectrum are combined in the precisely proper amounts, all the apparent color disappears from view, and the result is white. When all the lengths of the light waves, stated in inches, are added, the aggregate is .00001320. The word *white,* in Hebrew, is לבנים, and has the number equivalent of 132—another obvious verification for the authenticity of the science of gematria.

When the three primary colors in their purity and in equal proportions are placed on a wheel, the process of spinning the wheel changes the apparent color to white. It is the combining of

Red	.00000284
Yellow	.00000228
Blue	.00000188
	.00000700

The total of 700 represents the purity and perfection of the concept of white. It is also the number value of *"He who sits in the heavens,"* ושב בשמים, 700.

The visible white light from the sun, when the wave length of each of its colors is stated, using the British inch, bears the numbers of the Elohim.

Red

284   *God (Theos),* Θεος

2840 *The God of our fathers,* ο Θεος των πατερων, (Acts 3:13)

2840 *I form the light, I create darkness; I make peace, and create evil; I the Lord do all these things,* עשה כל אלה
      יוצר אור ובורא חשך עשה שלום ובורא רע אני יהוה, (Isaiah
      45:7)

Orange

248   *The image of God,* בצלם אלהים

Green

2080 *The Most High,* υψιστου

Blue

1880   *The Most High, υψιστος*

188   *The beauty of Jehovah,* בנעם יהוה

Violet

164   *God the Great King,* אל מלך גדול

The range of visible light, using the inch, would be .00000284 minus .00000164, which equals .00000120. The number 12, the foundation number, is the active agent in creation. Photosynthesis is only possible because of the 12-fold symmetry of the chlorophyll molecule, the life-giver that transforms light into organic substance. Similarly, the range of visible light can be seen as 12 divisions, beginning with the three primary colors, red, yellow and blue, as shown below.

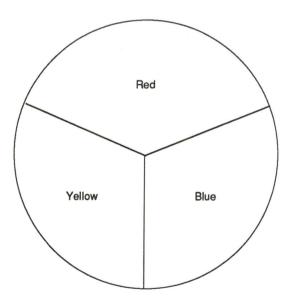

THE SIGN OF THE RAINBOW

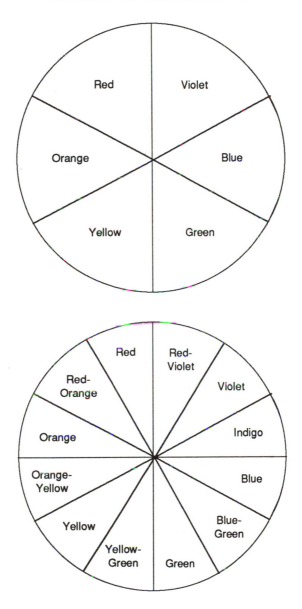

These 12-fold colors are merely the blending of the 3 primary colors. The spectrum, however, is generally stated as the 6 obvious colors of the rainbow: red, orange, yellow, green, blue and violet.

The rainbow, the sign of the covenant, was not only a promise that there would never again be a flood to cover the earth, but intrinsic within its refracted light from the sun, was the *sign* of the Creator, the circle, and the evidence of his light and power in the work of creation.

In the book of Revelation we are shown another rainbow. This rainbow is a complete circle around the throne of God.

> *...and I beheld a throne was set in heaven, and one sat on the throne...and there was a rainbow around the throne.* (Revelation 4:2, 3)

The word *"rainbow,"* ιρις, used here has the number equivalent of 320. When the solar number, 864, is divided by the common denominator of light, 27, the result is 32—the rainbow.

Those who bowed before that throne were saying, *"Holy, holy, holy, Lord God Almighty,"* αγιος, αγιος, αγιος, Κυριος ο Θεος ο παντοκρατωρ, 3898. When 3898 is divided by 27, the common denominator for light, the result is 144.370370370 to infinity, representing the completed work of creation (12 x 12 = 144) and the Creator, the Elohim, 37.

If 3898 were the circumference of the rainbow, the diameter would be 1240—a number relating to *time,* עד, 124, and the speed of light. *Light,* φως, 1500, multiplied by *time,* 124, gives the speed of light, 1860, (15 x 124 = 186).

The number 124 is filled with meaning. Its gematria in the Bible takes us again to that glorious topstone of the Great Pyramid—"The Light"—for *"a precious cornerstone,"* פנת יקרת, bears the number 1240 (Isaiah 28:16). It is also the number for *"Jehovah my God,"* יהוה הוא אלהים, 124, (Psalm 100:3), and it is the number for the perfect garden home given to Adam—

Eden, עדן, 124.

A square with sides of 124 has a perimeter of 496—a number that beautifully describes God's realm. The prophet Habakkuk gave us a word picture of His glory: *"His glory covered the heavens, and the earth was full of his praise; and his brightness was as light, and rays (bright beams) from his hand,"* (Hab. 3:3, 4). What a beautiful description of the glory of the Elohim. It sounds like a description of the rays of the sun, shining upon the raindrops, spreading its glorious colors across the sky, engulfing earth and sky in its circle of color. The phrase, *"His glory covered the heavens,"* כסה שמים הודו, bears the number 496. His description of *"rays (bright beams) from his hand,"* קרנים מידו לו, also bears the number 496.

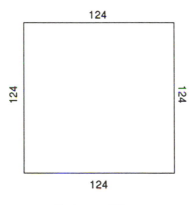

124

124

124

124

Perimeter 496

Habakkuk's complete description of the manifestation of the glory of the Elohim has a number equivalent of 2922. If this were the circumference of the rainbow, the diameter would be 930, representing the distance that light travels from the sun to the earth.

Man had been on the earth 1,656 years before Noah entered the Ark and the flood waters came. It marked the ending of an era and the beginning of a new era—one with a covenant of promise, as shown by the rainbow. The rainbow, spreading the light from the sun in a circle that engulfed the earth, connected the sun (God) and earth (man) in the covenant. The solar number, 864, when combined with the earth number, 792, totals 1656—the number of years from the breaking of the first covenant to the establishing of the second—a covenant of hope through the promise of salvation.

7

When the Answers are Simple, Then You Hear God Talking

Albert Einstein, as a young man, had a quest for knowledge. His work of a lifetime was the unfolding of the heart of knowledge, like the opening of a simple, yet beautiful flower, petal by petal. In 1905 he published his famous papers, *The Electrodynamics of Moving Bodies,* in which he showed that energy and mass are equivalent—$E=mc^2$. It was the drawing of the universe together by joining light to time; time to space; energy to matter; matter to space; and space to gravitation. His theory of relativity forced the revision of all fundamental thinking about time and space.

Einstein's response to nature was that of being in the presence of something God-like. He talked a lot about God, and his questions about the works of God were simple questions. He came to realize, through his life work, that when the answers are simple, too, then you hear God talking.

One of the simple truths that Einstein observed is that whether you are dealing with time, space, matter or energy, the speed of light is inextricably involved.

To acquire the speed of light forces time to stop. A simple, but crude illustration would be to observe the clock on the wall that says 12:00. Then move 186,000 miles away from the clock at the speed of light—it will take one second. But, looking back at the clock we see that it still says 12:00. It has not changed, because it takes the beam of light from the clock exactly the same length of time to travel 186,000 miles.

The Bible clearly tells us that *"God is light,"* therefore he dwells in eternity, which has no progression of time.

Einstein made simple the mystery of creation and its origin, within light. In his formula, $E=mc^2$, he told us that matter and energy are equal and interconvertible through the common denominator of light. His formula was for the converting of mass into energy. However, we can reverse the formula and state it as $m=E \div c^2$, thereby converting energy into mass—the basis of creation.

I have shown in chapter 5 the numbers basic to the formula. E equals energy—the power of the Elohim; therefore it is represented by the number 37, which is basic to the concept of the Elohim. c^2 is the speed of light squared, which is $186 \times 186 = 34596$, resolved to 27. Using these numbers in the formula, mass becomes 1.370370370 to infinity—the same as the physical constant of the hydrogen atom.

Hydrogen is the most basic and simplest of the elements. Its one proton in its nucleus is orbited by one electron. The proton in the center has a positive (+) charge, and the electron which orbits it has a negative (-) charge. The perpetual orbiting of the electron is due to the fact that as fast as it is moving away from the proton, the electrical attraction (+-) draws it in. Therefore it never stops.

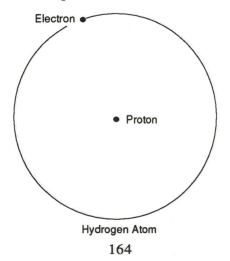

Electron

Proton

Hydrogen Atom

WHEN THE ANSWERS ARE SIMPLE

A hydrogen molecule is the inter-orbiting of two electrons around their respective protons; the orbits thus overlap as in the overlapping circles that formed the vesica.

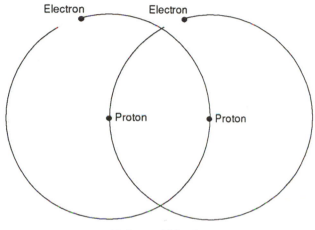

Hydrogen Molecule

The fusion of these two hydrogen atoms is the source of all heat, light and life in the universe.[1] The power of the hydrogen bomb is a small example of the tremendous amounts of energy stored in the hydrogen molecule.

Our sun is composed largely of hydrogen. It thus becomes a dynamic representation of the Elohim. The fusion of its hydrogen glows red in the sky. Even the numbers in the gematria for *red* are the same as the numbers for the Elohim; and the length of the red light wave in the spectrum is .00000284 of an inch—the number for *God (Theos)*, Θεος, is 284.

---

1   The fusion of the hydrogen molecule creates helium. The two electrons which had orbited their respective protons in the two atoms of the hydrogen molecule, now join in orbiting the two joined protons, as one unit. This process of fusion formed all the elements found in nature, and is the process by which the man-made elements are likewise produced. Thus all matter can find its source in the hydrogen atom, which represents God.

165

The struggle between "science and religion" has always produced its skeptics and visionaries. While many scientists question the existence of God, the more they search into the laws of the universe, the more they come to believe. Yale physicist, Henry Margenau, co-editor of *Cosmos, Bios, Theos,* concluded that there is "only one convincing answer" for the intricate laws that exist in nature: creation by an omnipotent, omniscient God.

An article in Time magazine (December 28, 1992), referring to atheism as a denial of the existence of God, posed the question: "If you admit that we can't peer behind the curtain, how can you be sure there's nothing there?"

We can, in fact, peer behind the curtain, and Einstein's theory of relativity is the very beam of light through which we can peer. What we find behind the curtain is beautiful beyond all human imagination, and in perfect accord with the laws of physics—we find the ultimate origins of matter and energy; and we do indeed find God!

Appendix

Miscellaneous

During the course of study for a work of this kind, it is only natural that many related items of interest arise, that do not specifically pertain to the subject being presented. Below are a few such items for the enjoyment of the reader.

Lights and Perfections

In the Old Testament we are given the information that the high priest, Aaron, wore a special breastplate as part of his official dress; and on that breastplate were two unique items, called the Urim and the Thummim.

> *And thou shalt put in the breastplate of judgment the Urim and the Thummim; and they shall be upon Aaron's heart, when he goeth in before the Lord.* (Exodus 28:30)

The purpose of the Urim and Thummim was for communication. Apparently Aaron was able to determine by these, whether his God was telling him "yes" or "no." But what were they?

The Hebrew words mean "lights" and "perfections," but beyond that, definitions fail us. Or do they? What about the gematria of these two mysterious items on the breastplate?

257   *Urim* (lights), אורים
  6   *and,* ו
490   *Thummim* (perfections), תמים

The total thus equals 753.

$$\begin{array}{r} 257 \\ 6 \\ \underline{490} \\ 753 \end{array}$$ plus *colel* equals 754

A circle with a circumference of 2368 (*Jesus Christ*, 2368) has a diameter of 753.7, or rounded to 754. It is interesting that *colel* is used here, and it appears to be for the reason that the true diameter of the circle is neither 753 nor 754, but somewhere between the two.

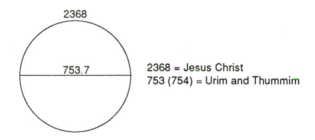

2368 = Jesus Christ
753 (754) = Urim and Thummim

What does the Urim and Thummim have to do with Jesus Christ?

Another reference in the Old Testament to the Urim and Thummim tells us that, after the priesthood had become defiled, they would not properly eat of the holy things until they had a priest who possessed the Urim and Thummim. But there never has been one. To whom did the prophecy refer? Let's look at the gematria.

...they should not eat of the most holy things, till there stood up a priest with Urim and with Thummim. (Ezra 2:63)

168

888   *A priest with Urim and with Thummim,* לאורים ולתמים כהן

888   *Jesus, Ιησους*

The reference is clearly to Jesus Christ as the rightful priest who possesses *"Lights and Perfections."*

Light from the Sun

The rounded figure of 93 million miles is generally used as the mean distance that light comes to the earth from the sun. If that mean distance were stated in inches it would be 5,892,480 (with, of course, many zeros, which have been dropped). Divide this by the speed of light and the result is 3168, the gematria for *Lord Jesus Christ.*

$$93 \times 63360 = 5,892,480$$
$$5,892,480 \div 186 = 3,168$$

Now let's take that same inch-measurement and divide it by the circumference of the earth. The result is 2368, the gematria for *Jesus Christ.*

$$5,892,480 \div 24,881.392 = 236.8$$

Finally, using the mean distance from the sun to the earth in inches, divide by the diameter of the earth. The result is 744, the gematria for *"two great lights."*

$$5,892,480 \div 7,920 = 744$$

He's Number One

It has been demonstrated that the Unity of the Elohim (Father and Son) are represented by the number 1. Below is a demonstration of the use of 1 in the Bible. Note the progression of 1s by using zeros merely as place holders. The Greek and Hebrew characters are not shown for reasons of space. More than one title per number is separated by a semi-colon.

0001 *A (alpha)*
0010 *To be exalted*
0011 *Earth; Gold*
0100 *A great God is Jehovah; The Most High*
0101 *Michael; Royalty; Great is the glory of Jehovah*
0110 *My servant David (Jesus); Your King (Jesus)*
0111 *Wonderful; The Most High; The Lord of all*
1000 *Lord; Everlasting power*
1001 *Testimony (of Christ); The sure mercies of David*
1010 *Great wonders*
1011 *Heaven and earth; Your Redeemer, the Holy One of Israel*
1100 *The throne; Unexcelling greatness*
1101 *The Creator of the ends of the earth*
1110 *Only Son; The root of Jesse (Jesus)*
+1111 *Name of the Son; Husbandman (God)*
─────
8888 *He must reign until he has put all enemies under his feet.*

Stonehenge stands lonely and silent in the morning mist.

Photo by Robert Alexander

171

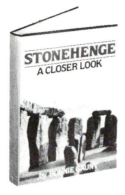

The Magnificent Numbers
of the Great Pyramid and Stonehenge

by Bonnie Gaunt

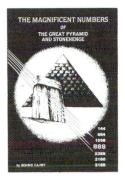

Numbers have long been a source of fascination and wonder to man. The ancient Pythagoras was so awed by the relationship of numbers to time and space that he theorized: "Numbers are the language of the universe."

The two 4,000 year old wonders of the ancient world, the Great Pyramid and Stonehenge, reveal their long-kept secrets by the correlation of their magnificent numbers—the numbers of the universe—and give us an insight into their purpose, their architect, and their relative importance to modern man.

Paperback, 214 pages, fully illustrated
$10.00
Postpaid in the United States

Order from:
Bonnie Gaunt, 510 Golf Ave., Jackson, Michigan 49203, U.S.A.

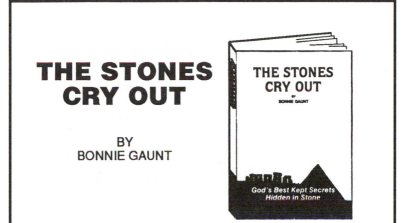

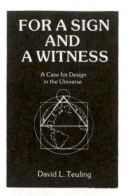